MW01633487

The Cradle Will Rock

The Cradle Will Rock

An Original Screenplay

Orson Welles

Edited & Introduction by James Pepper
Afterword by Jonathan Rosenbaum

Santa Barbara • Santa Teresa Press • 1994

SANTA TERESA PRESS
1980 CLIFF DRIVE
SUITE 224
SANTA BARBARA, CALIFORNIA 93120

FIRST EDITION
Limited to 1000 copies
ISBN 0-944166-06-7

PRINTED IN THE UNITED STATES OF AMERICA

The production of
this book is for
Lindsay Anderson

INTRODUCTION

James Pepper

You are about to experience the principal achievement of the last year and a half of the life of Orson Welles. The screenplay for Welles's intended production of *The Cradle Will Rock* is invigorating, quickly capturing the reader with its winning charm. Sharp, warm, introspective, humorous, life embracing, and calmly perceptive are but a few of the other adjectives that can be applied. For those wondering about Welles's creative abilities toward the end of his life, this screenplay is offered up as a major accomplishment. It fans afresh the burning energy found throughout Welles's work.

It is tempting to try to take this wonderfully written blueprint and attempt to mentally picture the images of the unborn film that Welles might have sculpted from it. But such dreamy thoughts are especially illusionary with Orson Welles, a director who always kept pushing himself stylistically; what does remain is a remarkable script written by a vigorous filmmaker with his creative batteries still fully charged.

This screenplay is unique as an autobiographic probe by a man nearing seventy, restricted in his work by cumulative circumstances, looking back at himself nearly a half century earlier. It is a vision of a young Orson Welles caught up in a torrent of flowing creativity who had not yet made any major mis-steps in his professional career. The year 1937 was a time before Welles's phenomenal reputation and the ensuing myth became the juggernaut that overran him. *The Cradle Will Rock* film project provided Welles a moment for self-reflection and not all that he saw in his earlier self he found he liked or tried to justify. Turning to his real life colleagues he created their portraits with wise observation and considerable kindness.

The Cradle Will Rock is also a look at a time unique in the American theater when our government took a direct role in regionally spreading the professional stage by sponsoring the Federal Theater through the New Deal's Works Progress Administration. The 1937 censorship problems involved in Welles's staging of Marc Blitzstein's proletarian opera *The Cradle Will Rock* have their contemporary echo in today's struggle over the funding granted through the National Endowment for the Arts. Franklin D. Roosevelt's massive use of the federal government apparatus to reverse the depression had begun to stall by the time of the opera's production. Salaries of WPA workers in the arts programs had been cut and the Federal Theater received closer scrutiny. An opera sponsored by the government that dealt with the exploitation of steel workers, the manipulation of the church, the potential murder of a labor leader, and the subversion of the press was a heady mixture for combustion.

Why Welles did not manage to film his account of that dramatic time will be shown by Jonathan Rosenbaum in his afterword. It should be noted that it is the one motion picture project in the last years of Welles's life that came the closest to being produced. The single event that overshadowed and crippled Welles's working life from the 1970s on was his failure to complete his much anticipated film, *The Other Side of the Wind,* which was shot and roughly assembled. That picture, at this writing, still sits in storage encumbered by legal and financial problems. Taken out of Welles's hands, the series of events involved were ultimately not of Welles's making nor under his control. The failure to complete *The Other Side of the Wind* became a lightning rod for renewed criticism of Welles with devastating effect. The damage done to his ability to function in the world of film was starkly recorded by Welles himself in an eleven-page letter written from Los Angeles in 1977 to Medhi Mouscheri, President of Astrophore Films, the largest single investor in *The Other Side of the Wind*:

> . . . My own first priority, for much too long now, has been "THE OTHER SIDE OF THE WIND." Tragically, very little of that time has been spent on constructive work. Overwhelmingly, it has been time lost in simply waiting for the *chance to work* — time utterly wasted. Weather in the movie business is highly changeable. The market itself fluctuates quite wildly, and my "market value" both as a performer and film-maker has slipped to the lowest point in all my career.
>
> The [American] Film Institute "Tribute" [presenting their Life Achievement Award in 1975] dramatized the presumed advent of "THE OTHER SIDE OF THE WIND." That picture, so eagerly looked forward to, has failed to appear. And for me, professionally, that failure has been mortal. As a director, my reputation by now appears to have been blackened beyond reparation. In this industry — in this small town — two things are said of me today. "That picture isn't finished yet — the Crazy Welles . . ." and "No use offering him a part, he'll turn it down; he doesn't want to work."
>
> The "Tribute" should have been a turning point. It certainly created for me a notable renewal of interest on the part of the Hollywood Community. During the year that followed, and for several months after that, I received any number of film, theatre and TV offers — all of which I turned down. What I could have accepted (without any conflict in time) comes — according to [Arnold] Weissberger's [Welles's agent and attorney] documentation — to something more than two million dollars.

> I sacrificed all this, as you know, in order to keep myself free for the completion of our film . . .
>
> I have been in the performing arts, working for my living, for some forty-seven years. I have never been rich. In this rather ridiculous business we learn to sustain ourselves on hope and enthusiasm. So I've never been really poor.
>
> But today I find myself not only without income, but without prospects. With my professional credit destroyed, it's not too easy—in the sixty-second year of my life—to make plans for a fresh start. . . .

Welles was down at that moment, but certainly not out. The life and power of *The Cradle Will Rock,* written seven years after this letter, match the energy of the characters and events it portrays. An angry or artistically defeated man could not have written it.

Those unfamiliar with Orson Welles's early career might find a brief outline of his life up to 1937 useful. He was born in 1915 in Wisconsin and early showed a precocious aptitude for the arts. His mother, an accomplished pianist, taught him piano. At age three, he made his dramatic debut with a walk-on appearance in *Samson and Delilah* at the Chicago opera house. At eleven, he entered the Todd School for Boys in Woodstock, Illinois run by Roger Hill, who encouraged Welles, allowing him to direct, design, adapt, and perform in plays and promoted his interest in magic. After graduation, Welles spent a brief sojourn at the Chicago Art Institute before he left for Ireland on a sketching tour. Welles quickly convinced director Hilton Edwards to make him a member of the Dublin Gate Theatre acting company. Starting at sixteen, Welles rapidly gained noticeable attention as an actor in productions like Maugham's *The Circle* and Shakespeare's *Hamlet.* Outside the Dublin Gate he appeared in numerous other plays, including works by Ibsen, O'Neill, Shaw, Chekov, Shakespeare, and others. Returning to New York in 1933, the eighteen-year-old Welles, through the aid of Thornton Wilder and Alexander Woollcott, met director Guthrie McClintic and actress Katharine Cornell, who engaged him for their extensive national tour of *The Barretts of Wimpole Street* and *Candida.* Welles began his work in radio during this period, a career which quickly gathered speed with his work for CBS and NBC including Welles's own adaptation of *Hamlet.* Welles's star potential crystallized in his fiery role of Tybalt in Cornell's 1934 stage production of *Romeo and Juliet,* In November 1934, Welles married Virginia Nicholson. Archibald MacLeish's blank verse drama *Panic* starred Welles in early 1935 and he met for the first time its producer, and his future partner, John Houseman. The founding of the Federal Theater allowed Welles his first major triumph as a director with an all-Black cast production of *Macbeth* starring Jack Carter in the title role. Set against a voodoo background, the play created a sensation and toured seven federal theaters. Continuing his radio work, he directed and starred in a Federal Theater production of the eccentric farce *Horse Eats Hat.* Marlowe's *The Tragical History of Doctor Faustus,* staged by and starring Welles, followed in another innovative production in January 1937, again sponsored by the government. During this time, Welles received the major radio role of the mysterious crime fighter, The Shadow, which he played for two years. In June 1937, a twenty-two-year-old Welles and his associates attempted the opening of the Federal Theater production of Marc Blitzstein's opera, *The Cradle Will Rock.*

Screenwriter and director Philip Dunne once remarked that Orson Welles was incapable of a dull act. *The Cradle Will Rock* presents an intriguing collective portrait of diverse professionals striving to do their best work during a unique period of the American stage. They are helmed by a young master artist flexing his creative gifts and exhibiting his stunning sense of showmanship. But all is not joyous youth; there are the quiet hints of the deep frustrations in Welles's life that are to come. Whether his screenplay is read as autobiography, theatrical history, or purely as a dramatic work, the experience is of paramount importance in fully understanding Welles as a man and an artist. As Welles's last completed screenplay, *The Cradle Will Rock* is an inspiring testament to a potent filmmaker still in full creative harness straining at the reins.

• • •

For the fullest account of the troubled production of *The Other Side of the Wind,* the reader should turn to Barbara Leaming's *Orson Welles—A Biography* (New York: Viking Press, 1985). The book was written with Welles's direct involvement and contains much autobiographical material. The other great source of Welles's autobiographical views is to be found in *This Is Orson Welles* by Orson Welles & Peter Bogdanovich—edited by Jonathan Rosenbaum (New York: HarperCollins, 1992).

The editing in presenting this screenplay has been extremely minor, consisting largely of clarifications of directions or an occasional intent. This book has most carefully reproduced Welles's use of line spacing and breaks within speeches, which he used to indicate pauses or brief passages of time.

The research and aid in producing this book is spread among people separated by great distances. Oja Kodar graciously granted permission for Welles's screenplay to reach a larger audience. Alfred Shapiro contributed greatly to this book's appearance through his support and enthusiasm. James Curtis, more than anyone else promoted the publication of this work, eagerly giving his fine advice and friendship. The following individuals are all also to be thanked for their contributions to this book: Lindsay Anderson, Frank Beacham, Peter Bogdanovich, Simon Callow, Harry Carey, Jr., Marilyn Fix Carey, Philip Dunne, Michael Fitzgerald, Kim Geary, Gary Graver, Henry Jaglom, Dave Kehr, Bill Krohn, Todd McCarthy, Sasha Newborn, Deborah Sanford, Jim Steinmeyer, Peter L. Stern, Alessandro Tasca di Cutò, Beatrice Welles-Smith, Bart Whaley, and the late Richard Wilson.

James Pepper

The Cradle Will Rock

1. There exists a real treasury of PHOTOGRAPHS recording the desolation, anguish and the curious beauty of Americans standing up straight in the midst of that long storm we remember as the years of our Great Depression . . . The MAIN TITLES . . . and the visual background of most of the OPENING NARRATION will feature a significant selection of these photos.

2. SERIES OF SHOTS: NEW YORK STREETS—NIGHT

ORSON WELLES'S VOICE

This happened (and it really did happen) in the midst of the Great Depression. Franklin Roosevelt was President and one third of the nation was ill housed, ill clad, and ill nourished. He said that. And he was right. But misery seemed to draw us together. There never was a time when people were so nice to each other. Even a tough town like New York was like a friendly little village. Here comes Mrs. J. Sargeant Cram (who really existed) cruising the streets in her Rolls-Royce . . .

3. The headlights of the limousine pick out some wretched people trying to sleep on the pavement. A cruel wind is blowing. (The action is as Orson Welles describes it.)

When she sees some homeless person crouched on the sidewalks (and they're easy to find) she stops and sends out her footman with a stone— (the Rolls is full of stones). Close to each person the footman leaves a wad of wet money, and places a stone on it so the wind won't blow it away . . . We'll learn a little later why the money happens to be wet . . .

By now the footman (with the chauffeur to help) has finished doling out money to this particular band of derelicts. The car is about to start.

MRS. CRAM

(whose dignity is simple and authentic even if she does look like George Washington in drag)

Stop. Do you hear that, Jason?—a peculiar noise?

JASON

No, Mrs. Cram.

MRS. CRAM

I do: it sounds like a horse dancing. That wouldn't be likely, would it, Jason?

JASON

No, Ma'am, not likely at all.

MRS. CRAM

Listen carefully—

CHAUFFEUR

Yeah . . . now you mention it. Seems to come from that old van.

The old van in question is very old indeed. Somebody long ago has stolen its wheels and it teeters on blocks . . . The Chauffeur turns the car so it faces the open back end and shines his spotlight on:

4. INTERIOR. THE VAN.

A neat, elderly figure prancing about inside the van is rendered motionless by the sudden glare of the light. This is SOLLY PRUETT. Unlike many who sleep on the streets, he is neat as a pin and closely shaven with a tiny moustache which seems to be cut out of a shoe string. After a moment of mutual surprise MRS. CRAM speaks:

MRS. CRAM

(*to her footman*)

The creature is dressed entirely for July. Quick, Robert—

THE FOOTMAN hurries out with an offering. MR. PRUETT, up in the van, is in a commanding position. Very courteously he refuses the money.

MRS. CRAM

Sir—

MR. PRUETT

Yes ma'am?

MRS. CRAM

What do you do for a living—Or rather, what *did* you do?

MR. PRUETT

(*with some pride*)

I was a specialty.

MRS. CRAM

Were you indeed?

MR. PRUETT

Clog dancing, ma'am. I was only practicing just now—

MRS. CRAM

Call me Mrs. Cram.

MR. PRUETT

I'm Mr. Pruett . . . Solly Pruett.

MRS. CRAM

Clog dancing, Mr. Pruett?

MR. PRUETT

Vaudeville, Mrs. Cram. Clog dancing on the four-a-day—the Gus Sun Time.

MRS. CRAM

I have a young friend who directs plays for the WPA. Take this card to him at this address.

She gives the card to ROBERT, the footman, who takes it to MR. PRUETT.

MR. PRUETT

He needs a clog dancer?

MRS. CRAM

I cannot say, but he'll sign you on in his theatre. So keep the money, Mr. Pruett—as an advance against your salary.

MR. PRUETT

Mrs. Cram, I'm sorry, but I'm afraid you're making this up.

MRS. CRAM

Why should I?

MR. PRUETT

It's a lot of money . . .

MRS. CRAM

It will get you a place to sleep and some warm food—

MR. PRUETT

But it's *charity*—

MRS. CRAM

That's not a dirty word, Mr. Pruett. Are you religious?

MR. PRUETT

No, ma'am.

MRS. CRAM

Neither am I. But you know what the Bible says. "Though I understand the mysteries and all knowledge, and have not charity, I am become as a sounding brass or a tinkling cymbal. For now we see through a glass darkly," etcetera.

MR. PRUETT

That's fine for the ones that do the giving. Some of the rest of us have our pride.

MRS. CRAM

Too bad for you.

MR. PRUETT

Yes, ma'am — isn't it?

DISSOLVE:

5. SERIES OF SHOTS:

ORSON WELLES'S VOICE (continued)

One of Mr. Roosevelt's ideas was to get people out of the free soup kitchens and put them to work, and to pay them for their work. That was the WPA which included, among other things, our first and only National Theatre.

This is the story of a strange event which took place in nineteen thirty-seven in one of these theatres on Broadway in New York.

To those who may find the character of Orson Welles a rather outrageous improvement on the original, the director of this film would like to make it clear that this is no accident.

6. MARC BLITZSTEIN could be described as fine-tuned rather than highly strung. His is the attentive stillness of some birds: one of the predators — a gyrfalcon. Serious rather than solemn, he brightens a room when he enters it. His political beliefs are like moral convictions but they are held with the most perfect serenity. In the Church he would be called saintly. A total stranger to extravagance in any form, he is mannerly, widely educated, unaffectedly civilized, a man of natural authority and unstudied charm. If he sounds a little too good to be true, he is, almost, just that. It never occurs to him that his mere presence is a kind of rebuke to the rest of us. This is our author-composer, the young man who wrote

THE CRADLE WILL ROCK.

Tonight he is meeting for the first time the very young man who will direct this opera. It is, in fact, the late afternoon on a matinee day when MARC approaches the WPA theatre called "Project 891" where ORSON WELLES is playing in his own production of MARLOWE'S "DOCTOR FAUSTUS."

6. STAGE ENTRANCE — (MEDIUM FULL-SHOT) — DAY

MARC opens the door, is confronted by MR. PRUETT in a jester's cap and bells. MARC explains himself and is admitted.

7. INTERIOR. BACKSTAGE—(SERIES OF SHOTS)

All but blinded by several different kinds of hellish smoke, MARC struggles to gain the iron stairway leading to the basement of the theatre (which has been indicated by a frenzied assistant stage manager . . .). He is impeded by a terrifying parade: THE SEVEN DEADLY SINS . . . gesturing in various attitudes, mad and obscene, they float by in the spooky air . . .

8. FRESH ANGLE: MARC'S VIEWPOINT FROM THE WINGS

On the stage: FAUSTUS awaits his final hour—his damnation.

FAUSTUS

See, see where Christ's blood streams
In the firmament!
One drop would save my soul.
O, I'll leap up to my God!
Who pulls me down?

Music and effects—
(Just at this moment they are quite horrendous.) Then silence.

9. FRESH ANGLE: FAVORING MARC

Serious, impressed, he tiptoes down the iron stairway to—

10. INTERIOR. THEATRE BASEMENT (UNDER STAGE)—(SERIES OF SHOTS)

Filled with the mysterious machinery used for working the illusions above. The effect down here is more magical than what's happening onstage . . . These dark, devilish engines are manned by a crew of half-crazed veterans with faces out of Daumier . . . Just now they are—(considering that they're New York stagehands)—very curiously intent . . . Above them, on the underside of the stage floor, a pattern of small holes has been drilled through the boards. Through these, tiny shafts of colored lights play through the gloom picking out from among the old men here a watchful eye, there an attentive ear. . . . MARC, approaching the first of these ancients to ask where he might "locate Mr. Welles—?" chokes himself into silence when he hears a slow, whispered counting:

"One . . . Two . . . Three—"

MARC becomes aware that every stagehand is whispering a separate count, and thus managing some separate mystery. Occasionally, pacing footsteps blackout one set of peepholes or another. On different numbers each stagehand moves some part of his machine, at which, evidently, something splendidly strange takes place on the stage above.

A sudden, a quite terrible noise turns MARC in a new direction where he can just make out a frenetic little band whanging away on sheets of iron, giant gongs and clusters of oversized chimes. Clearly, FAUSTUS is being called to his account . . .

A wild cry from onstage, and an explosion of living flame fills the entire theatre, like some huge satanic firework. And now, through a fresh attack of yet more sulphurous smoke, a tube of asbestos leading down from above is seen to shudder. A rude sound of quick unzippering—and ORSON (as FAUSTUS) steps forward, holding out his hands.

ORSON

Marc Blitzstein—?

They shake.

I read the script last night—got through the score this morning. It's a wonder, Mr. Blitzstein—just a perfect wonder! Follow me—

He vanishes into the smoke. MARC hurries to catch up.

CUT TO:

11. EXTERIOR. STAGE DOOR—(SEEN FROM INSIDE TAXI)—LATE DUSK

MARC is hustled into the cab, followed by ORSON.

ORSON

(*introducing the cab driver*)

This is Marc Blitzstein, Moishe—the famous composer—

MOISHE

Never heard of him. Take the cold cream.

As he passes it back we realize this is New York rude, no special offense intended. In fact, MOISHE is one of ORSON's "regulars" . . . The cab fights its way through the late-afternoon traffic, ORSON larding himself with cold cream and rubbing his face briskly with the towel.

ORSON

(*his voice somewhat muffled*)

Moishe, three months from now—less—the whole world will be talking about this man's opera—

MOISHE

And you're the one that's gonna stage it for him? Hey, Blitzstein! There's a red light—open the door, jump out, run like hell—

MARC

(*cheerfully*)

In what direction, Mr. . . . er . . .

MOISHE

Carnegie, the Metropolitan, Sam Harris—Minsky's for Godsake—wherever.

As the taxi squeals to a stop, ORSON lowers the towel and confronts MARC with the beaming face of a twenty-two-year-old boy.

ORSON

Come on, I've got some groceries to earn—

He jumps out of his robe and the taxi in practically a single movement. He looks fine running toward the broadcasting building—except that his trousers are still rolled up to the knee (to accommodate the FAUSTUS costume).

CUT TO:

12. INTERIOR. RECORDING STUDIO

All are watching the big clock, ready and waiting for ORSON. At the last possible moment the entrance door flies open, and ORSON, smiling cheerfully at everybody, strides briskly to the mike . . . Spooky music and effects.

ORSON

(*fiendish laugh*)

Who knows what evil lurks in the heart of man . . . The Shadow knows!

(*fiendish laugh*)

MUSIC UP . . . STORM . . . Then down for:

SHADOW ANNOUNCER

The Blue Coal dealers once again present radio's strangest adventurer—

While the ANNOUNCER is speaking, MARC is absorbed by the sight of AGNES MOORHEAD (who plays THE SHADOW'S SECRETARY) on her knees, unrolling ORSON's rolled-up trousers. ORSON gives her a big kiss, and takes the script—obviously the first time he has ever seen it. He will have to pick up the story as he goes along.

SHADOW ANNOUNCER (continued)

. . . the mystery man who strikes terror in the very hearts of lawbreakers and criminals. Tonight Blue Coal brings you . . . The Shadow!

MUSIC UP and down.

We get a glimpse of the control booth, where MARC, carrying ORSON's sketch pad, is being ushered in and given a seat.

12. INTERIOR. RECORDING STUDIO

ORSON

Crime does not pay . . . The Shadow knows!

CUT TO:

13. INTERIOR. 891 THEATRE—PORTAL LEADING TO "LADIES POWDER ROOM"

JOHN HOUSEMAN, Administrator-in-Chief of this WPA project, stands waiting with stifled impatience for the last of the females from the matinee to get out and leave the place free for other purposes. He carries some folders under his arm and sports the bow-tie he is destined to make famous. Now in his early thirties he conveys an impression of greater age by virtue of a magisterial air, wholly natural and unforced, and already impressive.

MRS. MAYZIE KATZ enters the scene and circles HOUSEMAN on her way into the washroom. She seems to have passed through the wringer a number of times, but is charming in a wild and scattered way. She sounds crazy but knows a hawk from a handsaw.

MRS. MAYZIE KATZ

You're Houseman?

HOUSEMAN

Yes.

MRS. MAYZIE KATZ

This *is* the ladies' can?

HOUSEMAN

(*politely*)

Yes, Madam.

MRS. MAYZIE KATZ

(*after studying him for a moment*)

I won't ask you what you're doing here, lurking at the door. That's your affair.

She goes briskly through the door into:

14. INTERIOR. LADIES' POWDER ROOM

DISCOVERED: AUGUSTA WEISSBERGER, secretary to Project 891, hanging up the phone.

MRS. MAYZIE KATZ
(*as she enters*)
Where's Orson Welles?
(*turning on HOUSEMAN as he comes in behind her*)
You still here? You oughta be ashamed!

HOUSEMAN
I ought to have an office.
(*to AUGUSTA*)
Where is he?

AUGUSTA
Orson? He's doing "The Shadow" –

MRS. MAYZIE KATZ
(*uttering a wild cackle*)
"Who knows what evil lurks in the hearts of men?" . . .

AUGUSTA
And they just called from "The March of Time" –

MRS. MAYZIE KATZ
(*triumphant*)
And you know what that means – the *ambulance*!

CUT TO:

15. EXTERIOR. NEW YORK STREET (SECOND UNIT) DAY

A COP holds back traffic as an ambulance swerves around a corner and, siren screaming, speeds through a red light and away.

16. INTERIOR. AMBULANCE

MARC
(*struggling cheerfully to keep his place in the vehicle*)
Orson – ?

ORSON
Yes?

MARC
Why the ambulance?

ORSON

I hire them . . . I made an interesting discovery—There's no specific law that you have to be going to the hospital to ride in one.

The ambulance has come to a screaming halt. ORSON leaps out. MARC follows.

17. INTERIOR. STUDIO ONE AT CBS

A complicated SET-UP. Five sound effects men, a full orchestra and a lot of actors. MARC is partially hidden behind the base section. WESTBROOK VAN VOORHEES stands at the announcer's mike.

VAN VOORHEES

(*his hand to his ear*)

Early last evening, in his Florida estate—a few short weeks before his ninety-eighth birthday—death, as it must to all men, came to John D. Rockefeller, richest and most ruthless of the oil tycoons . . . Vilified by many whom he bested in the rough and tumble of big business, blessed by the many who profited from his philanthropy—large . . . and small.

The MUSIC segues from the funereal to the cute.

ORSON (ROCKEFELLER)

(*as the ninety-seven-year-old ROCKEFELLER*)

Sonny . . . Come on over here, young man, and look at this . . . What is it?

"YOUNG BOY" (a grown-up ACTRESS)

What ya got there in your hand, sir?

ORSON (ROCKEFELLER)

Well?

"YOUNG BOY" (a grown-up ACTRESS)

It's a dime, mister.

ORSON (ROCKEFELLER)

A dime—that's what it is. And what's it worth?

"YOUNG BOY" (a grown-up ACTRESS)

Ten cents.

ORSON (ROCKEFELLER)

Keep it, save it. Work hard and earn some more. Keep pilin' up those ten cent pieces, sonny—and some day—*you*'ll be rich!

MUSIC UP . . .

MARC, observing this from a discreet corner of the studio, is not impressed.

CUT TO:

18. INTERIOR. WHAT WAS THEN MORE COMMONLY CALLED "JACK AND CHARLIE'S"

The celebrated ex-speakeasy is the hottest eating address in town. (We won't identify it by name—or needn't—so no problem of matching) . . . ORSON and MARC are making their way past the throng at the bar. The CAMERA is low so we don't see most of the famous people exchanging greetings with ORSON. In some cases just backs of heads, in others they're seated so we don't see them at all.

FIRST MAN'S VOICE
Orson, how *are* you?

ORSON
Hi, Moss—*Noel!* I didn't know you were back—

FIRST WOMAN'S VOICE
We're coming to see you again Friday night.

ORSON
That's great. Maggie, Leland, this is Marc Blitzstein.
(*he spots someone ahead; respectfully*)
Good evening, Miss Barrymore.

SECOND WOMAN'S VOICE
(*the one and only*)
Good evening, Mr. Welles.

SECOND MAN'S VOICE
Darling! When can we expect your Julius Caesar?

ORSON
When we get it past the bureaucrats.

MARC, throughout all this, is a figure of quiet and impeccable dignity. It is impossible to tell whether this is his first visit to the snootiest saloon in the Western World—or not. He looks pleased but serious, and quite untainted by that reversed snobbery which might be expected from so dedicated a Marxist torch-bearer.

19. INTERIOR. THE RESTAURANT

MARC and ORSON are just seated at a "good" table when two huge and beautiful trays of seafood (lobster and crab, clams and oysters) are placed before them.

MARC

My! Doesn't that look marvelous . . .

ORSON

After your revolution, Marc—what are you going to do with a place like this?

MARC

(*smiling, and with perfect sincerity*)

A place like this . . . ?

He glances around, blithe as a bird at Maytime.

ORSON

Tear it down?

MARC

Nothing of the sort. We'll just build more of them. Many more . . . There'll be places like this for everyone.

ORSON stares at him . . . The serene and happy certainty of MARC's response is irresistible.

DISSOLVE TO:

20. EXTERIOR. THE THEATRE—NIGHT

ORSON and MARC go through the stage door.

And ASSISTANT STAGE MANAGER sticks his head in the doorway.

ASSISTANT STAGE MANAGER

Ten minutes, Mr. Welles.

21. INTERIOR. STAGE OF THE THEATRE DURING THE EVENING'S PERFORMANCE

INTERCUT:

MARC IN HIS SEAT
(Thus what is seen on stage is largely his viewpoint)

22. THE STAGE (SERIES OF SHOTS)

(A synopsized view of the play) . . . FAUSTUS, having conjured up MEPHISTOPHILIS (Marlowe's spelling!) visits the POPE'S COURT IN ROME. In full view of the audience (and without camera tricks) he is rendered invisible, and proceeds to play havoc with the banquet His Holiness is offering some Cardinals . . . Drinks are splashed in faces, food flies about in the air, and finally, the Pope himself is (by an invisible foot) kicked high, and scuttles away with his guests and servants in great disarray . . .

In another scene some lecherous old fellow scholars, having heard of DOCTOR FAUSTUS'S magical powers, ask him to produce for them "the admirablest lady that ever lived—Helen of Troy." "Gentlemen," says FAUSTUS, "be silent then, for danger is in words."

MUSIC . . . FAUSTUS opens his arms as though in a gesture of ritual, and out of the murk there appears HELEN OF TROY, high in the filmy air, as though riding on a cloud.

He looks up at her dark form and as he looks, takes wing and flies up, through the air to HELEN'S side.

FAUSTUS

O thou art fairer than the evening air
Clad in the beauty of a thousand stars!

Now, as FAUSTUS rises to her, HELEN is aglow with new light . . . We realize that she wears a mask. FAUSTUS, embracing her, raises the mask . . . Her head falls back, loosening a great fall of reddish blonde hair. It reaches almost to the ground above which she floats.

FAUSTUS

Her lips suck forth my soul—see where it flies!
Come, Helen, come, give me my soul again.

. . . The kiss is obviously real, and held for longer than is customary on the stage. The instant before a first titter might be heard, he drops her head—her body—

There is nothing there! Nothing but her cloak—

FAUSTUS himself falls down from the sky. He hits the floor hard. (It is almost like an accident.)

And now, at the sound of a tolling bell, he raises his head and we see he is no longer the young man (nor the mature scholar)—He is suddenly old . . .

This is the last midnight, the hour when Doctor Faustus must keep his dreadful bargain . . .

23. FRESH ANGLE:

MARC in his seat in the front row hears the same words which had come to him earlier today when he blundered into that witches' cavern under the stage.

INTERCUT:

24. FULL SHOT: THE STAGE

ORSON (as FAUSTUS)
Adders and serpents, let me breathe awhile!

25. CLOSE-SHOT: MARC IN HIS SEAT

THE VOICE OF FAUSTUS (offscreen)
Ugly Hell, gape not! I'll burn my books—

26. FULL SHOT: THE STAGE

THE IMMENSE CURTAIN OF FLAME RISES FROM THE GROUND AND FAUSTUS VANISHES.

27. CLOSE-SHOT: MARC JOINING THE GENERAL APPLAUSE

28. FULL SHOT: (FRESH ANGLE): THE STAGE

The house curtain is down; the principal actors come out through the center opening, ORSON and JACK CARTER (all in gold and black fur) last.

CAMERA PANS to MARC, seated in the first row on the side, MOISHE, ORSON'S more-or-less private driver, hurries down the aisle, grabs MARC and before the rest of the audience stops clapping, runs away with him.

29. BACK-STAGE

The applause ends . . . the stage lights cut off, and in their place a big work light descends, casting weird shadows . . . THE CAMERA picks its way through a jungle of Faustian props and giant puppets to reveal:

MAYZIE KATZ (the eternal intruder) conducting a one-woman behind-the-scenes exploration on tiptoe.

Suddenly:

ORSON'S VOICE
(*a hoarse whisper*)

Mayzie!

MAYZIE

OmyGod!!!

ORSON

(*appearing out of the darkness*)

What's wrong?

MAYZIE

Don't scare me like that!

ORSON

No need to horse around, Mayzie, this is urgent.

He abruptly turns his back on her.

Zipper!

MAYZIE

(*totally bewildered but full of goodwill*)

Zipper?

ORSON, who entered the scene with his cold cream and towel, gets hurriedly to work on his face.

ORSON

I'm afraid Virginia may have invited you to go with us to Harlem—

MAYZIE

Whaddaya mean "afraid"?

She pulls down the zipper and ORSON steps out of his robe, leaving it where it fell.

ORSON

Buckles. And go get Jack.

She falls to her knees and begins detaching the costume buckles from his shoes.

MAYZIE

Jack who? Houseman. That man won't *listen* to me—

(*suddenly struck with the idea*)

Jack *Carter*? I *adore* him.

ORSON

No, darling—you adore *me*.

MAYZIE

That's true. But just for a moment there, it slipped my mind.

ORSON

Try to retain this: Houseman and a little group of swells—Muriel Draper, Archie MacLeish and their ilk, have probably reached my dressing room door—which I have locked. The hope is that for a while they can be persuaded to think that I'm inside. Go—encourage this delusion.

After a blink or two she starts obediently away. (This entire scene is played in loud whispers.)

MAYZIE
(*stopping*)
Archibald MacLeish?

ORSON
The People's Poet—and editor of Fortune Magazine.

MAYZIE
And you don't want him up in Harlem?

ORSON
I don't want to *go* to Harlem.

MAYZIE
(*dashed*)
And your poor little wife?

ORSON
Don't call her my "poor little wife."

MAYZIE
She was so looking forward to a treat—

30. ORSON comes to a halt. MAYZIE has been chasing him as he makes his way behind the black velvet cyc and through more and even stranger scenery. (Although both are perfectly sincere, both, being actors, are "onto" each other and have been playing this as though they had an audience.)

ORSON
(*taking a watch out of his pocket*)
By this time they'll be breaking down the door. Cover for me. Tell Jack I'm taking Blitzstein to the country—

He starts away again, MAYZIE still in pursuit.

MAYZIE
Blitzstein would rather go to Harlem with the rest of us—
(*sweet-talking him shamelessly*)
Especially with *you*. Jeez! They call you "The King of Harlem," don't they?

ORSON
Two years ago, sweetie. 'Been a lotta kings since.

MAYZIE
Carter, for instance?

To this there is no reply.

He says there's going to be some kinda fabulous rent-party—

ORSON

So I hear. Should be a good one.

MAYZIE

And Billie Holiday's at the Apollo—

ORSON

(he has almost reached the stage door)

Ella . . . Willie the Lion's still at Small's.

HOUSEMAN'S VOICE (distantly offscreen)

Orson—

OFFSCREEN—SOUND OF KNOCKING . . . MAYZIE is close at his heels as ORSON leaps briskly out the door.

31. EXTERIOR. STAGE DOOR—NIGHT

Just as briskly, ORSON leaps into MOISHE'S waiting taxi.

MAYZIE

(to MOISHE)

For a guy to be so warm and loveable—he's gotta study, don't you think? He must have majored in smart-ass.

ORSON

(wreathed in smiles)

It just comes naturally.

CUT TO:

32. INTERIOR. THEATRE—HOUSEMAN, MACLEISH AND OTHERS (A SMALL GATHERING)

Grouped at the dressing room door . . . HOUSEMAN now knocking rather fiercely. JACK CARTER, in all his golden glory, has a dismaying effect as he enters scene.

JACK CARTER

I wouldn't do that—

HOUSEMAN turns to him, falling back very slightly.

He doesn't care too much for JACK but, gritting his teeth, manages an amiable introduction.

HOUSEMAN

This, of course, is Mr. Jack Carter, our Mephistophilis who, as you know, made a bit of Shakespearean history up in Harlem—

JACK CARTER

We played downtown as well.

HOUSEMAN

Indeed we did—

JACK CARTER

Probably the longest run that play has ever had on Broadway.

A brief, rather tense silence.

There was also a national tour . . . I was ill for a while and Orson took over the part. That was history, too: the first time a white actor in an all-Negro cast played Shakespeare in black face.

HOUSEMAN

And here we have Mephistophilis in gold-face!

Admiring laughter . . . HOUSEMAN turns back to CARTER.

I'd call that quite a step ahead, Jack—wouldn't you?

The cold grey eyes flash no reply to this bit of inter-racial politics. A barber-shop signal from an automobile horn in the street has caught his interest.

JACK CARTER

I think I'll break down the door.

A flutter of mixed reactions greets this. He pays no attention, and with a single kick, reveals an empty dressing room.

HOUSEMAN

(pink-faced with indignation at this tomfoolery, but still coolly authoritative as ever)

I should explain something about Orson . . .

He moves out of the little dressing room, joining the others.

He is Mephistophilis to his own Faust . . .

This is greeted with an interested murmur.

In Dublin, when he started in the theatre he was just sixteen and claiming to be what he is now—twenty-two. In effect, this was a pact with Hell; he sold his youth for grown-up glory. As a result of which we are inflicted with these flashes of that delinquent adolescence he appears to have bartered away.

33. ORSON'S SPEEDBOAT PULLING AWAY FROM THE DOCK—NIGHT

ORSON is at the wheel. MARC (not looking as cheerful as usual) is the passenger.

MARC

Isn't all this against some kind of law?

ORSON

All kinds of laws and damned expensive.

Already most of the city lights are at their back, and the atmosphere is quite abruptly rural and romantic.

ORSON (continued)

Commuting like this is one of the two vices Virginia says I can't afford. The theatre's the other.

MARC

Virginia is your wife?

ORSON

You bet.

MARC

(*after a moment's thoughtful silence*)

Is it because she thinks it keeps you from doing more radio—is that why your wife says the theatre's too expensive?

ORSON laughs.

ORSON

The speedboat's what she objects to.

MARC

Well . . . It's a nice surprise.

ORSON

Roaring up the Hudson—? We'd probably make it a bit quicker if we went by foot. That is, if we could walk on water.

MARC

And you can't?

ORSON

It's more tactful to pretend one hasn't quite the knack of doing it for any distance.

DISSOLVE:

34. EXTERIOR. ORSON'S HOUSE AT SNEEDEN'S LANDING—NIGHT

The CAMERA dwells on for a moment on the moonlit scene . . . The house is rather old and ordinary, but not tonight, not under the moon . . . The Hudson glitters below, and in the foreground is a small rock-framed swimming pool, almost circular and very dark. At the edge of this stand MARC and ORSON, all their clothes piled up behind them.

ORSON
(calling in that special voice people use when they want you to believe they have no intention of disturbing you)
Are you asleep, darling?

Silence . . . Then, in the upper floor a light goes on in a window, framing the head of a beautiful young girl. This is VIRGINIA.

VIRGINIA
(calling down)
Who's that you've got with you?

ORSON
(calling up)
A great new composer.

VIRGINIA
Blitzstein?

MARC
How do you do, Mrs. Welles.

VIRGINIA
Virginia, please . . . I read your opera. Orson sent it out this afternoon. Are you afraid of snakes?

MARC
Yes, Virginia.

VIRGINIA
So is Orson. The water moccasin—that's the one to look out for. The rattlers are a quiet married couple who live under the porch. *They* won't bother you a bit. With the moccasin . . . keep splashing. I'll come down and get some anti-venom ready for us all.

She closes the window . . . MARC and ORSON, after a silent little pause, jump in.

After a brief bout of rather noisy swimming, they stop, standing together on the shallow end.

MARC
This is quite some life you lead.

ORSON

(suddenly very serious; with a strange kind of intensity)

Listen, Marc—I'm *lucky*! You aren't a gambler?

MARC

No . . . ?

ORSON

My father broke the bank at Monte Carlo, and he taught me about luck. When the dice are hot, stay with the long roll—go the distance. Go with me, Marc. I'm riding on a red-hot streak of wins. I'm lucky!

A sudden, sharp cry—

Oh, my *God*—!

A tense silence.

The water moccasin . . .

MARC

(breathless)

He bit you?

ORSON

(cheerfully)

He just missed. You see, I'm on that red-hot lucky streak.

MARC gives ORSON a mighty splash right in the face . . . Then they fall abruptly silent.

Music is breathing out of an open window on the main floor of the house. VIRGINIA at the piano is playing an excerpt from "THE CRADLE WILL ROCK" . . .

In the pool the two listening heads are motionless . . .

DISSOLVE:

During which the MUSIC cross-fades to another excerpt from MARC's opera.

35. INTERIOR. THE LIVING ROOM

Pleasantly shabby . . . full of junk—books and music, an easel and all kinds of stuff that looks played with . . . A nice dog . . . MARC is swaddled in one of ORSON's bathrobes. ORSON is wearing another. VIRGINIA looks great in pyjamas.

MARC

She plays well.

ORSON

(*dropping his voice*)

The damn girl's very talented. Right now—(in the greatest secrecy)—she's writing a novel.

VIRGINIA continues to play for a bit . . . ORSON has risen and now fades quietly away. MARC looks at her . . . She's cool and calm, no special reaction.

VIRGINIA

(*breaking in*)

It has all our friends in it—Noel, Joe, Alex Woollcott—everyone thinly disguised.

(*wickedly*)

Everybody, that is—*except Orson.* He isn't in it at all!

MARC

By the way, what's happened to him?

VIRGINIA

Gone . . . He does it that way—no goodnights. He also takes a lot of little naps. You know—like Napoleon.

Silence . . . MARC stares intently into space.

MARC

Napoleon? Should I take that as some sort of warning?

VIRGINIA

Orson's tall; and he claims that all the dictators in history are short.

MARC

(*after a brief pause*)

I'm not afraid of him, you know.

VIRGINIA

(*looking at him*)

I shouldn't think you were afraid of anybody . . . But something bothers you—

MARC

(*with a little laugh*)

I guess I feel that something *ought* to bother me . . . Maybe it's you.

(*pause*)

We're going to be friends, aren't we?

They exchange an affectionate glance.

VIRGINIA

I'm sure of it.

MARC

Then can we be very frank? Is it too soon for that?

VIRGINIA

Go on.

MARC

Virginia—you do realize that the whole point of "The Cradle" is what it has to *say*?

VIRGINIA

(*after a beat*)

Oh, yes. I realize that, of course.

MARC

But you don't honestly agree.

VIRGINIA

How can I answer that? What do I know—?

MARC, without speaking, silences her. After a brief pause, she starts once more, but with another tone.

That's dumb, isn't it?

I'm a grown woman; I don't live inside an egg . . .

MARC waits for her to go on . . . Virginia rises.

Okay. The things that "The Cradle" tells us are wrong—*are* wrong. It's just . . .

MARC

You accept the problems; you don't quite feel ready to face up to the solution.

VIRGINIA

(*suddenly a little cross*)

Well, there's always more than one solution, isn't there?

(*she rises*)

Let me show you to your room.

MARC

(*after a beat*)

I guess that's what bothers me.

VIRGINIA

(*affectionately exasperated*)

Oh, Marc—! That Orson and I don't happen to belong to your particular club?

MARC

(*another beat*)

I was going to say that maybe neither one of you has quite grown up politically . . .

36. During this last VIRGINIA has been leading the way down the narrow hall of her house. At this point she stops at a door and opens it.

But that would have been impertinent . . . wouldn't it?

VIRGINIA

Ask me that when I'm a little older . . .

MARC is a born charmer, but here he's turning it up a little too high. He know he's gone too far, too fast. So does VIRGINIA. All the same she gives him a nice enough smile.

This is your room.

MARC

(*lingering at the door*)

I'm afraid you won't be all that happy to have me as a houseguest. I do carry on, don't I, like some boring kind of missionary—

VIRGINIA

Dear Marc, you're on a cannibal island; we'll have you for our breakfast . . . Sleep well.

She gives him a quick little kiss, and goes.

DISSOLVE:

37. THE DOOR OF VIRGINIA'S KITCHEN—NEXT DAY

Fog rising from the river . . . a cold and rather gloomy morning. VIRGINIA, shivering a bit as she tightens the belt of her pretty dressing gown, ties herself into an apron and starts to make breakfast. At first she doesn't notice MARC, in the living room, crouched under the stairs and muffled in one of ORSON's huge djellabas. She flicks on the radio.

A VOICE (*on the radio*)

Oh, my darling little fool—!
What is it you're afraid of?

MARC

Wasn't that Orson?

VIRGINIA

(*having switched him briskly off*)

Who else? He's had that girl in a rumble seat every morning for three weeks now. Score: zero. How was your bed?

MARC

Perfect. I must have overslept . . . Where *is* he?

VIRGINIA

Soap. Up to his ears in it at CBS.

Briefly, she opens the radio switch again.

GIRL'S VOICE (*on the radio*)
I feel so . . . *cheap*.

VIRGINIA
That's Mayzie Katz, a friend of mine.

ORSON'S VOICE (*on the radio*)
Cheap? Never—*never*—

VIRGINIA
That's his Ronald Coleman voice. Sounds more like Herbert Marshall to me.

ORSON'S VOICE (*on the radio*)
—You crazy little fool—!

Off goes the radio again.

MARC
Virginia—

VIRGINIA
Yes, Marc. What would you say to a Spanish omelette—
(*then, after a beat*)
What *would* you say to a Spanish Omelette—"Buenos dias"?

MARC laughs politely.
Coffee then?
(*pouring it*)

MARC
You don't really want to talk about it anymore, do you?

VIRGINIA
(*a bit startled*)
What?

MARC
(*almost ashamed*)
My opera.

A short, uncomfortable silence. Then suddenly:
Right after he'd read it Orson rushed it straight out here to you . . .

VIRGINIA
Yes . . . with strict instructions—I was to serenade you with seductive excerpts the minute he'd got you into the rumble—Excuse me, the pool . . .

MARC looks at her. Then quickly looks away.

He's been wooing you—You've already admitted it—Weaving his great web.

MARC

Why does he bother?

VIRGINIA

Why does a politician kiss babies?

(*then, earnestly*)

But he does really love your play—I mean, your opera—

MARC thinks that over.

MARC

"But."

VIRGINIA

"But"? What buts—I didn't hear any.

MARC

(*with a nervous smile*)

Maybe just a tiny echo of a "but." I felt it buzzing in the air.

(*thinking hard*)

VIRGINIA

Marc, dear, I was born deep down inside your "Cradle." So was Orson, if you want to know the truth of it. I wanted another kind of life so I married him—and boy, did I get it! But just because I've managed to climb out of there, and down from there—I don't really want to shake the whole Goddamn thing out of the tree.

She catches her breath again; blows her nose on a very small handkerchief, and utters a melancholy little laugh.

Please excuse the language . . . I've been keeping bad company.

MARC

(*after a beat*)

The theatre? You like it? You get down there very much?

VIRGINIA

I work in his damn theatre; didn't you know? I was the comedy bride in his comedy fucking farce.

Silence.

MARC

Were you good?

VIRGINIA

I got a lot of laughs.

CUT TO:

38. INTERIOR. THEATRE

ORSON
(yelling)

Augusta—!

A young lady ASSISTANT STAGE MANAGER approaches the footlights.

MILLIE

Yes, Orson?

ORSON

Let's get on with the auditions. Who's next?

MILLIE
(weakly)

Mr. Solly Pruett.

ORSON
(whispering, or rather mouthing the words so as not to be overheard by MR. PRUETT)

I did—NOT—put him on the call sheet—

MR. PRUETT

Mr. Welles, sir—I'm still a volunteer—

MR. PRUETT has moved forward during this to the edge of the stage. Here, searching the audience with his watery, unfocused old eyes, he starts dangerously to sway over the orchestra pit.

VOICES (in the audience)

Pruett! Look out! (etcetera)

ORSON

Mr. Pruett—*please*!

MR. PRUETT
(a bit crossly)

Alright, alright! After a whole lifetime I guess I know my way around a sta—

Here he does very nearly fall into the orchestra pit. Hands reaching up from below seize his legs firmly, saving him from instant death. The hands belong to MARC, who now clambers up on top of the piano, keeping the teetering old performer strongly in his grasp.

MR. PRUETT
(*to MARC*)

Who are you?

MARC

I'm Blitzstein: You're Pruett. What part are you going to read . . . or rather, sing?

MR. PRUETT

I don't read. I'm a specialty. Do you fellas know my number? It's a song called "I Miss My Swiss"?

MARC, still clutching the spindly, shaking old legs, turns and casts a wild look of appeal in ORSON'S direction.

MR. PRUETT
(*complete with "comedy accent"*)

"I miss my Swiss,
My Swiss Miss misses me;
I missed her in de mountains—"

(This last has been, in a manner of speaking, sung.)

ORSON

Can you fake it, Marc?

MARC

Sure.

He sinks from sight.

YOBO
(*a hoarse shout from the audience*)

Pruett! Step back!

ORSON

Upstage, Mr. Pruett, so we can see you better.

MR. PRUETT
(*as he—in a manner of speaking—dances upstage*)

Today I do it with the shoes, you understand, but this is a clog dance.

He waits for his intro—gets it, and starts off.

ORSON

Abe—!

ABE FEDER

I gotcha! I gotcha—!

A follow spot, complete with a surprise pink gel, falls on the clog dancer and follows him. (SOLLY is doing splendidly.)

JOHN HOUSEMAN, spruce and cheerful, and looking, as he so often does, as though he has just emerged from a lengthy bath in a nice hot tub, emerges from his nest in the ladies' powder room. He establishes himself in a commanding position and surveys the scene.

HOUSEMAN
(*brightly*)
Now then . . .

39. HIS VIEWPOINT: THE ORCHESTRA PIT

A swarm of heads clustered around MARC (at the grand piano) and ORSON (sitting next to him on the piano bench, but facing the cast). The muttering breaks off, and all heads look up:

40. THEIR VIEWPOINT ON HOUSEMAN AT THE RAIL (INTERCUT)

HOUSEMAN
(*after a beat*)
I'm sorry if I interrupt—

Various cries from most of the others protesting that he has done nothing of the kind.

HOUSEMAN turns and goes.

41. FRESH ANGLE: THE AUDITORIUM OF THE THEATRE

The various heads of all the rest of the cast line up along the railing like targets in a shooting gallery.

MARC'S VOICE
Houseman—!

A wild clatter on the keyboard interrupts him, as MARC scrambles to the top of the piano to give emphasis to what he has to say.

HOUSEMAN
Jack . . . please.

MARC
Alright, "Jack please"—if there's anybody on the stage—I can't see them, and they can't see me.

JEANNIE
(*quietly entering the scene*)
As it happens this is the only piano we have—

MARC
(*sweetly reasonable*)
Jack . . . it's just a piano. Can't a couple of guys move it up? We can all of us help—

HOUSEMAN

(*sweetly patient*)

Marc, they won't *allow* us to help. The merest *offer* of assistance and they'll pull the mains and black us out.

MARC

(*angrily*)

Oh, come *on*—

HOUSEMAN

(*sadly wearily, he speaks the final words*)

Union rules, Marc.

MARC

(*suddenly subdued*)

Oh.

HOUSEMAN

And before this evening's performance of "Faustus" begins, six or eight stagehands will perform—still on overtime—the identical labor in reverse . . .

JEANNIE, seated now somewhere on the main floor, has raised her hand.

JEANNIE

What's wrong with an upright?

TEDDY TOMMASCHEVSKI

Yeah! A little one, like in nightclubs?

ORSON'S VOICE

Where will you put it?

Everyone cranes to look.

MARC

(*after a stunned silence*)

Up in the air, out of everyone's way? Pull it up with ropes?

ABE FEDER

That sounds so nice, Blitzstein, I wish it would work.

HOUSEMAN

(*with slight severity*)

Who says it won't?

ABE FEDER

(*indicating ORSON*)

Ask the Genius.

ORSON

(*aside to Feder*)

What can I give you, Abe, for the sweet love of Christ, to let up on that tired little retread joke?

ABE FEDER

(*to the others, with a leer*)

They *called* him a genius just this morning—in Women's Wear.

ORSON

That's a reprehensible lie. It was Thursday, in the Brooklyn Eagle.

He was playing for a laugh, of course, and gets it. But MARC cuts it off dead with a crash on the piano. At this all eyes turn to the pit . . . MARC'S angry head makes its appearance in the usual place.

Sorry, Marc. The point is that for "Faustus" there's so much elaborate rigging up high—

ABE FEDER

(*breaking in*)

And one little nightclub piano would fuck up my whole light plot.

HOUSEMAN

I think I have an idea . . .

The theatre is hushed; MARC in particular looking chastened and attentive.

This very small, nightclub-type piano—

JEANNIE, AUGUSTA and MILLIE

Yes—?

HOUSEMAN

(*very deliberately*)

We rent it, of course; and before curtain time, we open that iron door in the back and very gently push it into the alley and . . . park it there.

A respectful silence.

ORSON

I don't want to be the one who has to tell you this.

HOUSEMAN

(*with his nicest smile*)

But you will all the same—

ORSON

I have to, Jack: We already checked with the cops; it's just like they do with cars: they'll tow our little piano away—every evening.

Mutinous noises rise at this from the orchestra pit.

HOUSEMAN turns back slowly, commanding the entire room.

HOUSEMAN

Then I'm afraid the whole thing boils down to one simple decision—which only one man in this theatre can make.

All eyes turn to ORSON.

ORSON

Ouch.

Muffled laughter, which HOUSEMAN quells with ease.

HOUSEMAN

Rehearsals for "The Cradle" cannot take place without doing gross injury to "Faustus"? Well, as he ceaselessly points out to me, both of these plays are uniquely the creation of Mr. Orson Welles—

He holds a meaningful silence . . . then punctuates it with a European-type shrug. The theatre is mute. Then suddenly, MARC speaks up, full voice:

MARC

(*with astonishing intensity*)

Jack! I'm afraid you're wrong!

Low mumble-mumble from everybody.

MARC

This really *is* Orson's theatre, isn't it?

HOUSEMAN

Well . . .

MARC

(*cutting him off*)

And we've all got to realize that both of these plays are Orson's children—and he's quite right to be fighting for them both.

HOUSEMAN

(*after a beat*)

Ah, but Marc—Now he must tell us which of his children he loves most.

After a moment, and with a fine exit line to get him off—JACK HOUSEMAN retires from the scene.

ORSON, reddening, watches him go—then suddenly sprints after him.

In a moment the entire theatre is treated to the alarums and discursions of a classic HOUSEMAN-WELLES difference of opinion. As an actor, trained to project iambic pentameter to the utmost reaches of large theatre galleries, ORSON is, inevitably, the noisiest, and therefore sounds the more aggressive. That HOUSEMAN is busily, but quietly, kindling these flames is not apparent from any distance. But the members of Project 891 are well aware that if ORSON can roar like a lion, JACK HOUSEMAN has a smiling mouth which "biteth like the adder."

It goes on and on . . .

MAYZIE, at the pit rail, just above MARC, begins—not very loudly at first—to pound rhythmically on the rail, as she chants:

MAYZIE

BooO-rinng! BooO-riing—!

MARC raises his head from where it had been despairingly at rest on the keyboard, and as MAYZIE continues with her chant, he quickly improvises a simple but catchy tune to go with it.

People all over the auditorium and from all sorts of places backstage (to say nothing of the gang in the orchestra pit) join in the rising choir:

BooO-riing!! BOOORE-Iiing—!

It rings and thunders through the building, MARC adding many a resounding flourish on his concert grand.

But suddenly he breaks off—The singers fall silent . . . All listen intently.

The battle in the Powder Room is mute.

That these two gladiators have actually done each other in seems most unlikely. And yet . . . ?

And now the question is settled. The two (still rather pink of face) appear together . . . There should be applause—(there *will* be applause)—

But for now THE TWO turn to each other and, in the most formal style imaginable, shake hands. This is done with more than a whiff of self-parody, and MARC, quickly catching the mood, begins a minuet.

This THE TWO dance together, briefly and soberly. And a quick finish brings a storm of applause.

DISSOLVE:

42. INTERIOR. MOISHE'S CAB—NIGHT

52nd Street . . . This is the high epoch of the little jazz joints. There are lots of little neon signs and the air is filled with the weird braying of many great little combos . . . MARC sits fretting in the back. It is raining hard.

MARC
(*after a pause*)
Am I supposed to just *sit* here?

MOISHE
Whatever's goin' on up there isn't for us, Blitzstein.

MARC
(*instantly curious*)
Up where?

MOISHE
The third floor of this building—

It should be noted that MOISHE (like CARTER) is a man of many accents. Just here, for instance, he should have said "thoid" for third. He didn't.)

MOISHE
Hey—!

But MARC has already jumped out of the cab.

43. INTERIOR. STAIRWAY OF THE OLD BROWN-FRONT

MARC mounting it . . . A sound of sobbing: a woman's voice.

44. INTERIOR. THE FRONT ROOM OF THE APARTMENT

An enormous figure, tall and very fat, all but blocks out the window where she is standing. This is the actress (presently "at liberty") Marion Warren Manley. She is blonde and wears an immensity of plum colored velveteen in something of the style of a dowager's opera cloak. Seated beneath her and clasping her hand is Mrs. J. Sargeant

Cram. Except for the feverish neon of the jazz clubs the room is in darkness.

MRS. CRAM

Marion . . .

MARION WARREN MANLEY

(*through a snuffle*)

Yes?

MRS. CRAM

You're certain, Marion?

MARION WARREN MANLEY

Yes, I do think it would be good for me. I think he'd . . . want me to go.

She turns her head by way of indication, and MARC turns in the same direction. In a flash of lightning he realizes that it is right next to where he has been standing (near the door) — a coffin. Flashing neons brighten the features of the late Mr. Manley.

MARC shoots away.

MARION WARREN MANLEY

But where is Dashiell Hammett, and Robert Benchley and . . . all those other people?

MRS. CRAM

They were here . . . all of them. They've gone because they thought you'd rather be alone —

MARION WARREN MANLEY

(*quickly*)

Oh, no — !

MRS. CRAM

(*rising*)

They'll be along later, I expect, to my house to hear Orson's opera —

MARION WARREN MANLEY

(*murmuring*)

Bob Benchley was saying something about Tony's — I heard him.

MRS. CRAM

I'm sure that was for later, dear. I'll let you freshen up.

A stately exit by MRS. CRAM . . . the widow, left alone with the remains of the beloved, moves to the coffin . . . Some thoughtful mourner has left a splendid orchid on his breast . . . The widow studies it for a moment, then plucks it off and pins it on her cloak.

MARION WARREN MANLEY
(*to him, and to herself*)
You would have wanted me to wear it, wouldn't you?

She teeters away.

CUT TO:

45. INTERIOR. MOISHE'S CAB—NIGHT

A disconcerted flicker of night-lifers, celebrated and otherwise, are dimly visible as they scuttle from the house of death to Tony's just across the way . . . MARC returns in some haste to the back seat of the taxi.

ORSON'S VOICE (offscreen)
Marc—

ORSON appears at the cab window.

ORSON (continued)
You should have stayed put in the car . . . This was only a caper of old Crambo, you know. She wanted to show Marion—(that's Manley the large lady with the dead husband)—that she has more caring friends than she thought she had. Our little run-through tonight was supposed to divert her from her sorrow; but as it turns out she's gone off with the caring friends to "Tony's." That leaves just us.

MARC
It leaves just you. I'm going home to my own apartment and get a good night's sleep.

ORSON
(*calling off*)
Jack—

JACK CARTER
(*joining ORSON at the car window*)
Not me, Boss man; you've shown me the corpse. That's enough fun for one evening—

ORSON
Stick with Marc—*please.* He's growing restive, and I've got to find the Crambo.

JACK CARTER
Where's Virginia during all this?

ORSON
(*as he drifts away*)
Yes, where *is* Virginia?

JACK gets in the cab next to MARC.

JACK CARTER

You're sore about his missing some rehearsals—

MARC

Am I supposed to be happy?

JACK CARTER

(*a slight flare-up, a little tough*)

You're supposed to know where he's spending his time. And why.

MARC

Where's that?

JACK doesn't answer . . .

He never goes to bed . . . Isn't he ever going to grow up?

MOISHE

I don't think he wants to . . .

MARC

Peter Pan?

Silence.

JACK CARTER

He gets down to Washington a lot. He's fighting for his theatre . . .

MARC is astonished.

"Faustus"—that's a real old play, right? More'n three centuries.

Slight pause.

The other day some redneck Congressman stood up and said the man who wrote it is a well-known communist . . . So how do you figure they feel about your opera? Orson is down there trying to cover your ass.

MARC

(*bewildered*)

Yes—?

MOISHE

Then, too, he's signing autographs. You know, like a movie star. Except he pays for them.

MARC

(*irritated*)

Pays who?

MOISHE

Fans. A dollar each.

MARC

(after a moment's thought)

That isn't true.

MOISHE

No, it isn't.

MARC

Then why did you say it?

MOISHE

(in what turns out to be his normal, educated voice)

Because I'm supposed to be one of these oddball characters that drives a cab in what they call a madcap comedy.

MARC

But you aren't?

MOISHE

I'm studying Oriental Languages at Columbia. I do the oddball character for Orson. That way he can pretend he's in the movies.

Silence . . . Then:

MARC

(wearily)

Yesterday he dragged me into some kind of ex-speakeasy full of chorus girls.

JACK

(to MOISHE)

Yeah . . . those guys are nuts about show business.

(to MARC)

There was a cat joined your table—remember? Controls a whole lot of that action. So all of a sudden let's suppose you need a whole bunch of the big green. And you gotta have it fast. Our young genius picks up the phone, and Charley—he delivers . . . But after that, naturally, Charley owns him.

MARC

(still tired, still cross)

Charley?

JACK CARTER

You read about him all the time . . . In the newspapers they always call him "Lucky"—Dig?—Like Luciano.

For good, intelligent reasons MARC looks a little scared.

MARC

Jesus — !

CUT TO:

46. INTERIOR. THE BALLROOM OF MRS. CRAM'S TOWNHOUSE

MRS. CRAM has not taken off her hat, but she has rolled up her sleeves. She stands behind a big bucketful of soapy water, and is working cheerfully away on a wash board. The time shows on the face of a grandiose clock on the mantlepiece behind her: three fifty-two in the morning. No wonder the music of "The Cradle" we are hearing comes not from MARC, long before this snug in his bed, but from VIRGINIA. By this time she knows most of the show by heart, and is doing full justice to it. MRS. CRAM and MR. PRUETT make up her entire audience.

She comes to the end of a scene.

MRS. CRAM

I have a building called "The Peace House" — has Orson told you about that?

VIRGINIA

Oh, yes, Mrs. Cram — often.

MRS. CRAM

He used to want me to turn it into a theatre, and I commissioned him to translate some of the Greek plays that have a bearing on the subject.

VIRGINIA

I think he ought to talk to you about that.

MRS. CRAM

Instead he's talking to my husband. Nobody ever does; and Orson never fails . . .

During this last MRS. CRAM has wrung out whatever it is she has been washing and has hung it with two clothes pins on a line strung across the ballroom. It is, unmistakably, a ten dollar bill . . .

On each side of it are other pieces of freshly washed paper money. The entire clothes line is aflutter with clean bills . . .

CUT TO:

47. MR. CRAM'S ROOM

This is our second encounter this evening with a horizontal ancient. MR. CRAM is motionless but alive. The large, dim, violet colored eyes still dance with a certain ghostly mischief. His beard is silvery, his brow serene and his vocabulary limited:

MR. CRAM

ChristGoddamnit—!

This is all he ever says.

ORSON

(chatting away, as he often does, with the old gentleman)

. . . As for the news—it isn't too hot. Madrid is still holding out, but in Chicago there was a helluva mess with Republic Steel—a lotta people hurt, and ten strikers dead. Seven of 'em shot in the back . . .

MR. CRAM

ChristGoddamnit!

Silence . . . Then:

ORSON

Have I ever mentioned Ned Sheldon? . . . Edward Sheldon, the playwright? . . . Can't write plays anymore. Much the same sort of fix that you are—Can't move an inch; but do you know what he does? He *rules* the American theatre. All the great and famous people come to him for advice. And live by his advice. He's like some fabulous wise man on a mountain top, an oracle.

Thornton Wilder paid me the compliment of presenting me to that oracle. I don't think there was ever a prouder day in my life. He phones me now after anything halfway decent I get to do on the radio and, of course, I bring him all my plans and problems in the theatre . . .

MR. CRAM

ChristGoddamnit . . .

ORSON

I don't suppose this can be very interesting to you, Mr. Cram. If you want me to I'll stop.

ORSON waits for a sign. The eyes don't blink. The curse is not repeated.

ORSON

For Marc, that opera you've been hearing is the most important thing on earth. You'd hate its politics — radical — nobody in town would touch it except us. Our theatre belongs to the government, but they get their money from Congress and since the last election they could stop us dead. Of course, I could defy them.

MR. CRAM

ChristGoddamnit — !

ORSON

Oh, yes. I might find *some* way to get the show on in spite of everything — and that could help to make the actors' careers — it would certainly save Marc's artistic life. Mr. Sheldon says yes — I'm on to a great project. But like every great project, he says, there's something wrong with it, and somebody will have to pay. The "somebody" this time would be our theatre — the people left in it, who could be punished. It might even turn out that I'm the one who has the most to gain. I could look braver than I am, and be more famous than I deserve to be.

MR. CRAM

Christ —

The young eyes turn so quickly to the old man that the curse is silenced.

ORSON

He showed me what I had to solve; but he wouldn't tell me how to solve it. "You're a politician" he said . . .

That's all that he would say . . .

ORSON takes MR. CRAM'S hand in his. Then, after a moment, moves to the floor.

Did he mean if I had scruples I'd know what to do with them?

slight pause; then:

ORSON (continued)

Good night, Mr. Cram.

He goes out, closing the door after him.

Another pause.

MR. CRAM

I'll be God damned!

CUT TO:

48. INTERIOR. THE FOYER OF THE CRAM TOWNHOUSE—EARLY DAWN

VIRGINIA and MR. PRUETT are already at the door waiting as ORSON joins them.

ORSON opens the door a bit and sees—

49. EXTERIOR. DARK STREET

An extremely decrepit wagon with an ancient horse to match is waiting for the traffic light to change.

50. Geysers of steam rise from the streets like djinns, dancing in the icy air . . .

ORSON

Look at that, would you—

VIRGINIA

(*blankly*)

The horse and cart?

ORSON

An endangered species. Where does it come from? . . . To what strange mission is it bound?

VIRGINIA is unimpressed. The light changes and the wagon creaks away.

ORSON

Wouldn't it be wonderful to sneak in at the back of that thing and go riding away in it through the night?

VIRGINIA

Don't be silly.

ORSON

Silly? Ah ha!

VIRGINIA

Ah ha, yourself; you'd much rather be home in bed.

ORSON

What did Chesterton say about adventure? Adventure, he said, is an attitude taken toward discomfort.

(*turning to PRUETT*)

Mr. Pruett—

MR. PRUETT
(*sketching a salute*)

Sir—

ORSON

Just on a whim, just for the fun of it, wouldn't you be willing to be silly?

MR. PRUETT
(*uncertainly*)

When I was young, Mr. Welles—

ORSON

You know what's the trouble with women?

VIRGINIA

Men.

ORSON

They're like cats—they don't like us to catch 'em being silly—
(*turning to the others without waiting for an answer*)
So they miss a lotta fun—

VIRGINIA regards her husband with a certain dangerous gravity . . .

MR. PRUETT
(*after the briefest of pauses*)

Good night all—!

VIRGINIA

Good night, Mr. Pruett—

MR. PRUETT

Good night, dear lady . . . and sir.

After sketching a kind of salute the old man opens the door and goes tottering away . . . VIRGINIA and ORSON follow him and over their shoulders—

51. EXTERIOR. DARK STREET IN FRONT OF THE CRAM MANSION

VIRGINIA
(*after a pause*)

He lives on the West Side; he's going to walk through the Park.

ORSON
(*worried*)

He should have waited for Moishe—We could have taken him.

VIRGINIA

He says he needs the exercise . . .

Silence . . . Then:

He mustn't ever be down and out again . . . don't you agree?

He must never be . . . unemployed.

ORSON broods in silence over the inevitable future of Mr. Pruett . . .

DISSOLVE:

52. ORSON'S DRESSING ROOM

MARC, during his years abroad, has acquired the continental habit of first, half opening a door, and then knocking on it. He is confronted with what, at first, seems a pathetic spectacle: ORSON slumped over his dressing table, his head buried in his arms, sobbing his heart out. In fact, he's been trying to catch a few minutes' sleep.

ORSON

(*his voice muffled*)

Curtain time is . . . what?

AUGUSTA'S VOICE (offscreen)

Forty-two minutes.

ORSON reaches blindly for a stick of Leichner's makeup and goes to work in a random sort of way on his face. ENTER (by a side door) AUGUSTA WEISSBERGER with a paper bucket of chopped ice. ORSON suddenly starts to *vocalize.*

AUGUSTA

(*slightly startled*)

Ooooh!

ORSON

(*mock ham*)

It is not for nothing that they called me the thunderclap of the Dublin Rotunda. Gussie darling, what *have* you done with Patrice?

AUGUSTA

I haven't laid eyes on him. My mother brought you some soup.

ORSON

Tell her God sees everything she does and writes it down in a book, and makes me three very double vodka martinis.

Then quickly, as MARC with PATRICE (the second assistant) appear at the door.

ORSON

Two of which are for Mr. Blitzstein, who, as you see, is approaching with Patrice.

(in another variety of mock ham, quoting "Trilby")

The old crowd once more foregathered. Jove! It's just like a play!

(raising his voice)

Lots of good stuff for everybody who's stuck in both plays—The Stage Door Deli, Patrice—

PATRICE

Lindy's is closer.

AUGUSTA

(on her way out)

Reuben's is better.

53. ORSON follows her as far as the stage.

ORSON

(to MARC, as he passes him at the door)

As for you, my beamish composer—You'll look a bit less like a wounded deer if you'd remind yourself what day this is.

MARC

(gloomily)

Not much of a day for rehearsals.

ORSON

Matinee! That's twice around the track with Marlowe for me—

(remembering)

Hey! And afterwards tonight it's high society—

MARC

I'm not even going to ask you what *that* means.

ORSON

One of the oldest families on this island—

MARC

I'm staying home.

ORSON

Home?

MARC

My apartment.

(*a short silence*)

I'd like to move back to town.

ORSON

(*after another silence*)

Whatever you say.

MARC

(*on the defensive*)

I just can't keep up with you.

ORSON

(*rather sadly*)

Neither can I.

MARC broods over this, and before he can answer:

A VOICE (offscreen)

Orson—!

MAYZIE KATZ appears distantly. At this ORSON instantly disappears (by means of a star-trap).

MAYZIE

(*squinting into the darkness*)

I thought that was Orson—

MARC makes no reply.

Well if *you* see him, say I'm sitting in the sun with Virginia in front of the scene dock.

She goes. ORSON rises—at first slowly, then, when he's sure the coast is clear—quickly by means of another trap door.

ORSON

(*during this*)

"They search me here.
They search me there.
Indeed they search me everywhere.
Is he in Heaven? Is he in Hell?
That damned elusive Pimpernel!"

(*he vanishes again . . . then reappears*)

Shall we join the ladies?

MARC

That might be quite a good idea.

ORSON

I know . . . I know what's coming now— (With a friend like you, who needs a wife?) I'm going to be accused of even more neglect—Virginia. Right? Don't lie, Blitzstein!

MARC

Well . . . since you mention it.

(*compassion rather than rebuke*)

By the time *we* got home the other morning it was full daylight . . . Don't you ever sleep?

ORSON

No.

MARC

She was up and waiting for you.

Silence.

I wonder how you would have felt about it if you hadn't found her there?

ORSON

(*after a beat*)

Waiting—?

You mean if she'd walk out on me?

(*thinking about it*)

. . . God! where would she go—back home?

(*somberly*)

Marc—the only reason she married me was to *get away* from home . . . I'm not too happy about that . . .

(*moving away, he does a little brooding on his own*)

I promised her the Great White Way, and glamour—and, you know—the whole megillah. And instead, when she got here we were splitting up Horn and Hardart's twenty-five-cent daily blue-plate special, half and half, and filling up with water and the free bread . . . That's why I knock myself out on the radio. It buys us the house in the country and the pool and stuff . . . But the truth is even now we're always just a day or so ahead of the Sheriff. My salary on the WPA is thirty-seven dollars or something—I don't really know because I've never tried to collect it.

A brief silence.

MARC

Why?

ORSON

You have to stand in line.

Before MARC can make any comment on this, he continues:

ORSON

We got married practically at the request of our puritanical flea-bag of a hotel; and you know what she said to the Minister? Practically on the steps of that cheesy little altar? "Reverend—" she said, "because of our youth we're being forced to do this in New Jersey, and it's all rather irregular, isn't it? What I want to know is—will there be any trouble if we want to get divorced?"

MARC makes no comment. ORSON starts toward the stage door. (VIRGINIA'S question has been on his mind since she first asked it.)

Jesus, Marc—you think I don't realize how tough it is to be a girl? . . .

He has reached the door.

And it's not so Goddamn easy to be me.

He opens the door, and stops there, turning to MARC.

She was just a child, you know, when we were married—a school girl.

MARC

(*smiling at his friend*)

And what were you?

ORSON

I was the first train out of town.

CUT TO:

54. EXTERIOR. STAGE DOOR AND BACK OF SCENE DOCK—LATE AFTERNOON

Big wooden packing cases for Faustus's props and costumes are piled in front of the scene dock doors. Here VIRGINIA, MAYZIE and MR. PRUETT have spread out some newspapers to sit on and are enjoying the wintery New York sun. VIRGINIA is working on a sweater for ORSON . . . There is a steady roar of traffic.

Muted voices are heard . . . then MARC and ORSON come out of the stage door. They stop on the shady side of the packing boxes and can't be seen by the knitters in the sun.

ORSON

(*as he opens the door*)

My world is just too random for her—too damn full of surprise. Don't forget that where she comes from the big excitement is the menfolk getting gussied up in pink riding coats to go fox hunting, for Christ's sake, where there aren't even any foxes! . . .

VIRGINIA has frozen—

Not so much because of what she has heard, but because of what she sees:

55. REVERSE ANGLE: VIRGINIA'S VIEWPOINT—NEW YORK STREET

A DILAPIDATED OLD CART with a spavined Roscinante in the traces has just been halted by a red traffic light. It is not at all the same wagon we have seen the other night, but it almost could be.

56. FRESH ANGLE: THE (CLOSED) ENTRANCE TO THE THEATRE'S SCENE DOCK

VIRGINIA puts down her knitting and jumps into the street. Not pausing for an instant, she starts briskly toward the horse and cart. (ORSON drifts back inside the theatre and misses this.)

MAYZIE

Virginia—!

MARC

(following ORSON, has given him just time enough to catch sight of VIRGINIA)

Orson—!

MARC hurries back into the theatre and can be heard calling once again . . .

No reply. Obviously, ORSON has nipped quickly, so MARC reappears at the stage door just in time to see:—

57. HIS VIEWPOINT

VIRGINIA approaching the wagon.

CLOSER ANGLE:

VIRGINIA

(to the DRIVER, an ancient blackamoor)

Excuse me—

THE DRIVER

Yes'um.

VIRGINIA

Would you mind giving me a lift? I'll be happy to pay—

A VOICE (*from inside the cart*)
Begob, if it isn't an angel down from the sweet blue heaven itself! Give her a hand up, Rastus—

58. INTERIOR. THE WAGON

Mounted on the driver's bench VIRGINIA can now see that the voice belongs to a sexy young man, stretched out on the straw in the body of the cart.

VIRGINIA
Thank you.

The traffic light has changed: the cart starts up.

THE YOUNG MAN
You should be gettin' the curious benefit of the ice.

VIRGINIA
The what?

THE YOUNG MAN
Ice, me darlin'—lovely and cool, down under the layers of straw.

He holds out his arms invitingly.

VIRGINIA
It's very pleasant up here, thank you—
(*breaking off*)
I simply don't believe this man's name is Rastus!

(All the same, she's enjoying herself.)

CUT TO:

59. FRESH ANGLE: THE STREET OUTSIDE THE STAGE DOOR—DAY

As MARC watches, ORSON is dashing after the retreating wagon.

60. INTERIOR. THE WAGON

A slightly winded ORSON opens one of the gunny sack flaps on the side of the wagon (he is running along trying to keep up with it).

VIRGINIA
Dear, Mr. Kildare is an ice sculptor—

She indicates the startlingly beautiful young man (whose wardrobe suggests the peasant heroes of the Abbey Theatre) stretched out on the straw in the back—something of an early Brando in manner.

This is my husband, Mr. Kildare.

ORSON
(*breathless*)
Where are you going?

THE YOUNG MAN
Sure, and isn't it to one of them grand balls they're after throwin' in the name o' charity—for Mrs. August Bel*mont.*

ORSON
She's dead.

THE YOUNG MAN
Begob, what a shock that'll be for the Four Hundred—*And* for *Mister Belmont.*

ORSON
He's dead, too . . . Virginia—I don't think this man is any kind of sculptor at all.

She smiles at him.

THE YOUNG MAN
Well, sor, in the crool meejum of ice, sor—

ORSON
(*cutting him off*)
I'm onto you! I know who you are! . . . And *what*!

The wagon speeds up leaving Orson behind—

61. EXTERIOR. STREET

The following has something of the air of a soliloquy, but MARC is approaching.

ORSON
(*partially catching his breath*)
. . . All the creatures of the earth are male and female—Except us. There are *three* Goddamn sexes—men, women—and *actors*!

MARC
(*who has moved halfway toward ORSON in the street*)
Is there really an actor inside that thing—with Virginia?

ORSON
Well, I know damn well he isn't an *Irishman*!

VERY QUICK (VERY BRIEF) FADE OUT.

QUICK FADE IN:

62. THE STAGE—(SOMEWHAT LATER THE SAME AFTERNOON)

A very strange atmosphere indeed . . . VIRGINIA finds her husband standing thoughtfully on the Pope's banquet table . . . She waits in the shadows, watching, as the enormous pig (the centerpiece of the Papal dinner) rises slowly to its feet—its trotters, its hind trotters—and stands, apple in mouth, confronting ORSON . . . The pink nakedness of this absurd animal, and its very close proximity to the curiously absent-minded—the moonstruck magi—endows the scene with a strong hint of that muted obscenity which reigned over the "real magic" of the dark ages . . . A pause . . . ORSON has his arms around the pig (which stands almost as tall as he is). And suddenly we realize that the gesture is not intentionally erotic. It's a parody of the ballroom. These two are going to dance together . . . And they do—waltzing together high into the murky air . . . Then, in a movement almost too quick to follow, ORSON is astride the great beast, and completely motionless in mid-air. He looks down at his wife with the arrogant indifference of a stone condottiere in some forgotten piazza.

ORSON

I wasn't going to mention it, but there's a piece of straw on the back of your coat.

Before she can answer he begins to swing with his pig in great, graceful swoops around her, like a devilish carousel.

Been on a hayride, have you? And where to? East of the Sun and West of the Moon?

There has been music—(recorded music) though we weren't quite aware of it. Now there is a sudden, ringing silence. ORSON and his mount have halted again, waiting in front of VIRGINIA—frozen in space.

"Kevan Kildare" he calls himself—in summer stock.

VIRGINIA

Checking up on me?

He descends . . . he dismounts, leaving the pig gagging idiotically on its papier mache apple.

ORSON

Not really a bad actor. That much is true.

VIRGINIA

He's also a sculptor—a sculptor in ice.

ORSON

Edwin Booth said that an actor is a sculptor in snow.

VIRGINIA

You mean like snowmen?

ORSON

Or snow women . . . impermanent.

In a very gentle movement, feather-light, almost discreet, ORSON rises, all on his own—rises and moves through the air . . . He stops—his face in profile.

"Come, Helen, come—give me my soul again."

He is waiting (as in a dream) for the embrace of Helen of Troy.

VIRGINIA

(*unimpressed*)

You remember last night—when you looked at that old wagon? You were carrying on about adventure—

ABE

(*a loud cry from somewhere up in the flies*)

Ready, for Chrissake?

ORSON

(*yelling back*)

Yes, Goddammit!

HOUSEMAN

(*his voice, calling*)

Orson—!

ORSON

(*coolly, as FAUSTUS*)

"O, thou art fairer than the evening air,
Clad in the beauty of a thousand stars."

During this last HELEN has slowly materialized out of nowhere, and has floated down toward ORSON.

63. REVERSE ANGLE: THE AUDITORIUM OF THE THEATRE

(HOUSEMAN background)

MAYZIE

Oh, my God! How does he *do* it?

Wonderstruck, she moves down the center aisle toward the stage, HOUSEMAN behind her.

64. THE STAGE

As he speaks, ORSON has reached the stage level.

HOUSEMAN'S VOICE (offscreen)

Orson—!

ORSON
Look closely — She's angle-proof.

HE SNAPS HIS FINGERS: SHE VANISHES.

65. REVERSE ANGLE: HOUSEMAN

I've got to talk to you.

66. THE STAGE

ORSON
(*sarcastic, but hurt as well*)
You haven't bothered to notice what's been happening here?

67. REVERSE ANGLE: HOUSEMAN

HOUSEMAN
This is important.

68. THE STAGE

ORSON, in a sudden rage, plunges down the steps leading into the auditorium, CAMERA following him as he goes.

ORSON
I thought it was important to get Marc the rehearsal space he needs for his piano. This new effect replaces twelve square feet of special rigging. It also happens to be rather beautiful.

HOUSEMAN
I also have a bill for new money to be spent on an old production. "Faustus" has only nine more days to run.

ORSON
"The Cradle" has to be rehearsed; Marc needs his piano. And now he has it.

As he starts down into the auditorium, it can be seen that ORSON is carrying a sort of folding screen of oddly shaped mirrors. He holds it up a bit threateningly as he approaches HOUSEMAN, who turns coolly enough and moves away.

69. REVERSE ANGLE: A WIDE SHOT: THE STAGE

HELEN OF TROY floats to the floor level, and removing the mask turns out to be TEDDY. The beautiful lighting clicks off, the ugly work-light taking its place.

70. THE CENTER AISLE AT THE BACK OF THE AUDITORIUM

HOUSEMAN returning to his office in the ladies' powder room: ORSON following.

ORSON

And Jack, it's all done with these small pieces of glass—An elegant solution; and you—you don't even deign to look . . .

71. THE STAGE

VIRGINIA and MAYZIE glum-faced, watching this . . .

ANOTHER FAST FADE OUT.

Then:

FADE IN:

72. EXTERIOR. THE WELLES'S HOUSE IN SNEEDEN'S LANDING—NIGHT

Paper lanterns are strung out among the trees for VIRGINIA'S party . . . MARC is at the piano leading his people through one of the brighter scenes of "The Cradle." MR. PRUETT is in evidence, and we cannot help but notice on the buffet table, the two rough likenesses in ice of FAUSTUS and MEPHISTOPHILIS. The big French windows are open so this is easy to see and hear . . . A lamb is being barbecued in the foreground. Here a group of non-actors is gathered, somewhat older men and women with the confident air of the celebrated. ALEXANDER WOOLLCOTT is (as usual) by way of being Guest Number One. Also present are ROSE and BENNY HECHT, HELEN HAYES, CHARLES MacARTHUR and CALDER, the mobile sculptor.

GUEST NUMBER ONE (Woollcott, of course)

(*these foreground people are in silhouette and their dialogue is pre-recorded in L.A.*)

The show sounds quite amusing, but since our Boy Wonder seems to be sulking like whatshisname in his tent, I think I'll climb into my hansom-cab and go buckety-buckety back to Babylon for that supper with Harpo.

GUEST NUMBER TWO

Where *is* Orson, by the way—?

MAYZIE

(*nudging her way into the group*)

We think of him more as a guest of honor.

The others stare at her blankly . . . (Who is this woman?) . . . VIRGINIA enters the scene. (She stays a bit upstage in the light.)

VIRGINIA

Along with Jack Carter—who's always late. As for my husband—he's simply collapsed from exhaustion—

MAYZIE

(*breaking in again*)

And all those pills he's been taking to stay awake—

VIRGINIA

(*all serene*)

Let's just say he's drunk, Mayzie—it'll sound better.

MAYZIE

No, let's say he's a dope fiend, it's more picturesque.

GUEST NUMBER THREE

(*after a tiny pause*)

We like your new composer, darling; but where's he *been*? Nobody's even heard of him.

VIRGINIA

There was a longish stretch in Paris. He was one of Nadja Boulanger's star pupils. And then . . . well, he got married.

GUEST NUMBER ONE

And where does he keep her?

VIRGINIA

She died . . . not long ago—

MAYZIE

But not before she'd crammed him through a very heavy course in how to be a Marxist. So for Blitzstein, losing her sanctified the whole red ball of wax—a case of double-dyed idealism, if you see what I mean—

VIRGINIA

(*the good hostess—to the others*)

Like to hear another number?

Affirmative murmurs . . . The group has been sauntering toward the house and are now joining the cluster of actors and civilian guests by the piano.

VIRGINIA

(*delighted at his success*)

Marc, do Honolulu for us—please.

TALLULAH

(*shouting from some distance*)

Where's Orson, darling?

VIRGINIA

Up in our bedroom finishing some work. He'll be down any minute—

As MARC launches into the new scene—

CUT TO:

73. INTERIOR. THE BEDROOM

The "Boy Wonder" in pyjamas (which are just slightly too small for him) is peering out the window . . . He has caught sight of the SEXY YOUNG MAN FROM THE ICE WAGON. (Obviously VIRGINIA has been brazen enough to invite him to the party!) The sexy one
74. is doing himself well at the barbecue as ORSON watches—(the actor in him playing Othello) . . . But there's also a good deal of husbandly anguish . . . MARC'S piano and the VOICES OF THE ACTORS come loud and clear through the window:

ALDEN (Editor Daily):	Have you been to Honolulu?
HIRAM (Junior):	Are the women nice down there?
ALDEN:	Demure and so high-born, Just pure September morn.
HIRAM:	I don't care if they're high-born Just as long as they're high-breasted.
WILL (Mr. Mister):	Junior, please don't get arrested!
HIRAM:	La la la-la-la la. La la la-la-la la.
ALDEN:	Have you been to Honolulu?
HIRAM:	Sail away to that fair land—
ALDEN:	Dusky maidens in the starlight . . .

A sudden whizz of a sound, with much displacement of expensive gravel, signals the arrival of some tardy guest.

75. INTERIOR. BEDROOM

MAYZIE storms in.

MAYZIE
(*to ORSON*)

What are you *doing*?

ORSON

Doing? I'm not doing—

MAYZIE

There's supposed to be a party downstairs. It's been postponed a lot, but it's still in honor of the closing of "Faustus," and you were Faustus—

JACK CARTER enters as though he were a high-ranking police official conducting a raid.

JACK CARTER

Well, I'm Mephistophilis, and I'm here to say goodbye.

JACK wears a beautiful camel's hair coat and whatever else is visible is every bit as magnificent.

JACK CARTER

(*looking at ORSON*)

What's *he* doin' in *bed*?

ORSON

(*who hasn't turned at this*)

Resting . . .

Pause.

I'm desperately tired.

JACK

(*disgusted*)

"Desperately"—?!

JACK places a handsome lizard-skin boot on the small of ORSON'S back and—pushing rather than kicking—sends him flying off the bed.

Well, me—I'm just "desperately" fed up. Get your pants on, Maestro, before I feed you to the snakes.

ORSON

Why?

JACK CARTER

Why?

ORSON

Yes, why?
(Jeezus, I've got lousy lines in this scene)

JACK CARTER

This is our party. We got ice statues on the table, but if you're gonna go on pretending to be looney, the folks'll start thinkin' that old rumor was true.

ORSON

(*awakening for a moment from his stupor*)

What rumor? . . . You and me? Whoever believed that?

MAYZIE giggles.

JACK CARTER

About me and your wife.

MAYZIE stops giggling. ORSON, surprised, stares at JACK.

JACK CARTER (continued)
(*to MAYZIE*)

He's so dumb he has to use both hands to find his ass.
(*change of tone*)
I wish it *had* been true.

Slight pause.

But now the word's out about your Jewish pal—

ORSON

Marc and me? . . . Or Marc and Virginia?

JACK CARTER

The combination of your choice, Bubah.

ORSON props himself up so he can look through the window.

ORSON

It's that bastard down there—? She *invited* him—

JACK CARTER turns an inquiring look at MAYZIE. She shrugs.

MAYZIE
(*a parakeet screech*)

The no-good actor who's also a no-talent sculptor?

ORSON quickly closes the window.

JACK CARTER

You mean the cat that made the ice statue of me? Hey! he's pretty good.

During this MAYZIE has rushed over to where ORSON is kneeling at the window.

MAYZIE

All Ginny did was hitch a ride with him, shit-head—!

ORSON
(*to MAYZIE, a bit as though it were his dying words*)

Please—don't call her "Ginny."

JACK CARTER
(*his accent deteriorating with every word—a deliberate tactic*)

I ain't callin' her, or you—*period.*

MAYZIE

A very *short* ride—

JACK CARTER

See this black face? It's no longer available to lend that touch of savage Africa in offay society.

ORSON

(*momentarily sober and serious*)

What does that mean?

JACK CARTER

What does it sound like?

MAYZIE

(*to ORSON, at the top of her lungs*)

And she stopped for me—check it out—right on the corner of Twenty-ninth and Seventh Avenue—!

ORSON

(*after a beat*)

It sounded like you were quitting me.

JACK CARTER

You bet yo' sweet cheeks, Bubah—before I get fired.

ORSON

You're not quitting our *theatre*—?

JACK CARTER

All theatres. But yours is takin' on water fast, Cap'n; I'm just Rat Number One.

ORSON pays no attention, he is concentrating on JACK.

JACK CARTER

In our old joint up in Harlem, the commies are holdin' one of their sit-downs. And how much future do you reckon there is for a nigger Shakespearean on Broadway?

ORSON

(*to JACK, angrily*)

Don't talk like that—

MAYZIE

(*throwing a pillow at him*)

Two fifteen that afternoon—I was lookin' at my fuckin' wristwatch.

Putting the pillow on the window sill, ORSON buries his head in it.

ORSON

I'm tired, damn it! And overworked and under great mental strain . . .

And everyone's so abusive . . .

MAYZIE

Two-fifteen is when the fuckin' ice wagon hauls up where I'm standing. Check it out, "Bubuh"—Your wife gets out and joins me and we go off to the newsreel—

(*quick change of tone*)

Do you *realize* what's happening in Congress?

ORSON has turned sharply to MAYZIE, suddenly most attentive.

Look at him, will ya—?

She's reacting to the change in ORSON—pointing at him and appealing to JACK.

He doesn't give a shit for Congress. All "Bubah" wants to know is what happened in the sixteen minutes his wife was in that wagon finding out about sculpting ice, and hiring the stuff for this party!

She slams out of the room.

A pause . . . JACK, now in a comfortable chair, lights a cigar. ORSON still kneels at the window, staring out.

ORSON

I never had the slightest suspicion . . .

JACK CARTER

Just how old were you when you got married?

ORSON

Nineteen—since you ask.

JACK CARTER

Too soon for a bubble-head like you.

ORSON

So was she . . . nineteen.

JACK CARTER

Women are born older than we are.

ORSON

(*thoughtfully*)

Not that I've been as strictly faithful as I might have been—

JACK CARTER

(*rising*)

Okay, Maestro, goodbye—I'll be following your career.

(Can it be true that he's losing a friend?) ORSON gets to his feet.

ORSON

That really does sound like goodbye.

JACK CARTER

Do you give a shit?

ORSON

You know I do.

Their eyes meet.

Jack . . . how're you going to live?

JACK CARTER

High off the hog. Numbers.

ORSON

Level with me.

JACK CARTER

We're makin' a deal with the greaseballs.

(*after a moment*)

I'm gonna get rich, which means the trouble I get into I can afford.

A moment's silence between the two friends . . . Then JACK moves to the door.

JACK CARTER (continued)

You used to like it fine in Harlem. Come up for a visit now and then—while it's still fun . . . It won't be much longer.

He goes . . .

ORSON is alone . . . From below come bursts of laughter and sometimes even applause . . .

The music has stopped. He listens intently, not making anything out . . . After a time—and with an eye cocked on his mirror—he begins to speak:

ORSON

I don't think we've been introduced.

(*studies him for a beat*)

My name is Welles. Your name is Kevan Kildare, you are an unemployed actor, and I regret to say, quite a good one. You are here by invitation? . . . That would be Virginia . . .

Mirror, mirror on the wall—

ORSON raises his voice, in a sudden note of aggression:

What do I see? I see the best man in my profession under forty! That's what I am. That's what I see.

A nervous silence . . . Then:

They set up rigid standards for me before I could talk. Who the hell could live up to them? . . . And why do I keep telling myself that because I like people they like me? . . .

(*short pause*)

I try to console myself with unrequited friendships—

In the background, VIRGINIA has entered the scene . . . MARC, downstairs, has started some romantic piano music. ORSON catches sight of his wife in the looking glass.

ORSON (continued)

(*to her*)

I hear laughter and applause down there. Who's it for?

VIRGINIA

We've been playing The Game.

MAYZIE sticks her head in the door.

MAYZIE

Game? Which game?

VIRGINIA

Animals—"The Beastly Bestiary"—

It has to be people we all know, and you must describe them as mythical beasts.

MAYZIE

For instance?

VIRGINIA

Well . . . just for instance—who do we know who is like unto a newly born giraffe, with the sexy behind of a zebra?

MAYZIE

(*with sudden delight*)

I *do* have a sexy behind!

ORSON

(*to MAYZIE*)

And what a good cue that is for your exit.

MAYZIE

(*recognizing a command when hears it*)

I'll be waiting below.

MAYZIE vanishes — then instantly reappears.

MAYZIE

And now let's do Houseman —

VIRGINIA

(cutting her off rather sharply)

No. No, sorry.

MAYZIE

(being naughty)

Know what Virginia says — ?

VIRGINIA

Shut your trap, Mayzie.

MAYZIE

(like a bad little girl)

Virginia says —

ORSON

(interrupting)

Virginia has some crazy thing about Jack. She's wrong. It's just that lately he's a bissel peeved because I haven't let him watch rehearsals —

He takes MAYZIE firmly by the arm and leads her to the door.

I'm somebody he happens to need — And vice versa. In show business we call it friendship.

He closes the door on her.

A silence.

ORSON (continued)

(looking in the mirror again)

Now do me.

VIRGINIA

We always do you.

ORSON

Naturally.

VIRGINIA

The proud Arab steed again? . . . "He stamps the earth — his hot breath clouds the sky . . ."

She has ORSON'S fascinated attention.

MAYZIE

(at the door)

I've got it — ! Attila the Hun!

ORSON
(*to MAYZIE*)

Out! . . .

VIRGINIA closes the door on her with her foot . . . Standing behind ORSON, she catches his eye in the glass.

VIRGINIA
(*quietly, with a new note in her voice*)

Oh, yes . . . A one-eyed old circus bear dancing in the spring time to show us he's still young.

He looks at her. She meets his gaze.

VIRGINIA (continued)

But he was never young . . . that's his trouble, you see—he knows that we know that he was never young.

ORSON takes her hand. He speaks with a certain gravity and no sentiment.

ORSON
(*very seriously*)

And you—you are my little unicorn.

In a thousand years there has only been one of you—at one time.

VIRGINIA turns her head slightly to one side, studying him. The phone starts to ring—loudly.

VIRGINIA
(*a twinkle in her eye*)

You speak like a lasagna.

ORSON
(*picking up the phone*)

Now what the hell does *that* mean?

VIRGINIA

All sorts of layers . . . and the juicy stuff in between.

ORSON
(*into phone*)

Yes, Jack . . .

A pause while he listens.

Okay, we'll talk in the morning.
(*then quickly*)
Oh—sorry you couldn't come to the party . . . Night.

He hangs up slowly.

ORSON (continued)
(*to VIRGINIA*)

Houseman.

VIRGINIA

Bad news?

ORSON
(*grimly*)

He's been talking to Washington. They're really closing in.

VIRGINIA

Why don't you? Hopkins is supposed to be your friend—

ORSON

He is . . . It's that little gang of Neanderthals in Congress . . .

With his arm around her he starts to lead her out the door.

We'll talk about it later. Poor Marc's worried enough as it is . . .

They leave . . .

ORSON'S VOICE IN THE HALL

You think it's alright if I come down in my nightshirt?

MARC is still playing.

ORSON AND VIRGINIA'S VOICES
(*singing as they go*)

Have you been to Honolulu . . .

Dissolve:

THE DRESS REHEARSAL:

76. INTERIOR. THEATRE: THE STAGE—WITH SCENERY AND LIGHTING

A small audience scattered all over the auditorium (people connected in some way with the theatre project) . . . Full cast and choir onstage . . . full orchestra in the pit with LEHMAN ENGLE conducting . . .

The point has been reached for the scenery change into the HONOLULU NUMBER. Halfway through, ORSON, rising from his regular rehearsal seat in the ninth row, calls a halt. He moves down to LEHMAN; MARC, from the front row, joining a little discussion in which four bars are cut from the transition. LEHMAN turns back to the orchestra, ready for the downbeat—

HOUSEMAN

Orson—

ORSON freezes. This being a dress rehearsal with nerves frazzling all over, he manages, this time, to suppress his indignation at what he takes to be another unnecessary interruption . . . HOUSEMAN, very grim-faced, hands him a telegram. ORSON reads it quickly, putting it away just in time before MARC rejoins him.

HOUSEMAN

It's nothing, Marc—

ORSON

(*taking his cue from HOUSEMAN*)

Yes, just another bureaucratic botheration. Not to worry . . .

He moves quickly up the center aisle joining VIRGINIA in the back of the house.

ORSON (continued)

(*under his breath*)

This time it's an outright command—*We don't open period.*

VIRGINIA

What will you do?

HOUSEMAN has moved to ORSON'S side. They look at each other, speechless . . . Suddenly, ORSON turns back toward the stage, raising his voice.

ORSON

Taking five, Lehman?

LEHMAN

(*uncertainly*)

No . . .

ORSON

Then let's get on with it.

They do. With the full orchestra and choir it sounds beautiful; and as the illuminated platforms move and the neon moon rises over Honolulu, it looks extraordinary.

CUT TO:

77. EXTERIOR. THEATRE—DAY

A CLOSE-SHOT of CHAINS AND PADLOCKS being put into place by Officers of the Federal Government.

78. INTERIOR. THEATRE LOBBY—DAY

HOUSEMAN, JEANNIE, AUGUSTA, ABE and TED watching from inside . . . MAYZIE enters scene.

MAYZIE

Hey, guys—! The stage door is still open—

HOUSEMAN

(*irritated as usual by this noisy, nosey civilian*)

They aren't locking us in, you know. They're just locking out the public.

CUT TO:

79. INTERIOR. ORSON'S DRESSING ROOM—DAY

Raising his head, ORSON sees MARC in the looking glass.

MARC

Is it really true?

ORSON

Sure'n hell looks like it.

Then, after a stunned silence.

MARC

(*cross*)

Is that some kind of music out there?

ORSON

Will Geer and Howard Da Silva warming up. They've volunteered to entertain. The idea is to keep the audience from going home.

MARC

(*after a moment, thoughtfully*)

If they'll listen to Will, they'd listen to our show . . . What's to stop us from doing it right out there in the street?

ORSON

The cops. They'd break us up in a minute—

MARC

Because of what we have to say.

ORSON

Nothing political, Marc. Will and his guitar can be moved along. We'd be an obstruction . . .

Their eyes meet.

You'd be willing to give up your chorus, and all that scenery and the whole production?

MARC

Of course.

ORSON

Suppose we find some kind of a hall, or warehouse, or a church?

MARC

Or a theatre—

ORSON

(coming alive)

A theatre!—A real New York theatre!

CUT TO:

80. INTERIOR. THE POWDER ROOM—DAY

A small crowd is already filling the ladies' toilet. (More and more people will keep coming in throughout the following sequence.) AUGUSTA is on the phone. The theatre's second phone is ringing.

AUGUSTA

(into phone)

Project 891; just one moment please—

(into the second phone)

Project 891, will you hold on just a moment—

(appealing to the others)

What do I *say* to these people?

HOUSEMAN

(entering with TEDDY)

Who's calling?

AUGUSTA

Who's *calling*?—Everybody. What do I tell them when they want to know what kind of opening there'll be tonight in a padlocked theatre?

ORSON

Remember Carl Laemmle, the movie tycoon? He had a pest in his outer office who wouldn't go away. The problem, by lunch time, seemed insoluble. "He won't move," said the secretary. "What do I say?" "Give him an evasive answer," said Laemmle, "Tell him to go fuck himself."

(he turns to a little man seated nearby, an obvious stranger in a bowler hat)

Sir, I hope you'll overlook that rough word. I avoid that sort of language unless it's positively *imbedded* in an anecdote—

ORSON (continued)
(*to HOUSEMAN*)
A friend of yours, Houseman?

HOUSEMAN
No. He seems to have just wandered in.

THE LITTLE MAN
Correction, sir. You sent for me.

HOUSEMAN
Don't tell me you're Pratt?!

PRATT
Pratt's the name, theatre brokerage is the profession. *Arnold* Pratt.

ORSON
Well, sit right down, Arnold. You call me Orson, and speak frankly: is there — anywhere in this town — a theatre available for tonight?

PRATT
(*taking out his notebook*)
May I have the use of a telephone?

HOUSEMAN
(*who has already started dialing a number on the second phone*)
Go right ahead, Mr. Pratt.

PRATT
Arnold.

HOUSEMAN
Arnold.
(*his attention diverted by a reply on his phone*)
Hello — ?

ORSON
(*to PRATT*)
That's Houseman. You call him Jack.

TEDDY
I just want to ask one question —

ORSON
(*to PRATT*)
You call him Teddy.

HOUSEMAN
(*his phone still at his ear*)
Stop being silly.

HOUSEMAN (continued)
(to TEDDY)

What is it?

TEDDY

I just want to ask if it's occurred to anybody to do some checking with Actor's Equity?

HOUSEMAN

It's occurred to me. It's what I'm trying to do now—
(into phone)
Actor's Equity? John Houseman here; may I speak with Mr. Gilmore . . .

A tense silence. Then:
Oh? . . .

PRATT has dialed and reached his number.

PRATT
(into phone)

Francine? This is Arnie. Tell me, dear—what's dark tonight?

HOUSEMAN
(into phone)

. . . in ten minutes? I'll call back.
(hangs up)

PRATT
(the phone still at his ear)

Well, gentlemen, which would you rather have—the Lyric or the Gaiety?

ORSON

Both of them. They're beautiful—

MR. PRUETT

I'll take the Lyric.

MARC

Which one has a piano?

PRATT
(into phone)

What a shame.
(he hangs up; turns to the others)
The Lyric's out, there's a benefit.

ABE
(who has just entered)

We'll take the Gaiety.

PRATT

Closed for repairs.

MARC
(*to HOUSEMAN*)

Let's start with the piano—

PRATT

All the same, I think I've got an idea . . .

MR. PRUETT

He's got an idea—

HOUSEMAN meanwhile has begun to dial another number . . . A slight pause for this.

ABE
(*to PRATT, with some ferocity*)

Well—?

PRATT

Fifty-Ninth Street—how do you like that address?

JEANNIE

We love it, Arnold. What's the theatre?

PRATT

It's a big house, but it's cheap.

HOUSEMAN
(*turning from his phone*)

How cheap?

PRATT

The Seville Theatre, gentlemen. The best deal in town for that number of seats—

HOUSEMAN
(*into phone*)

Thank you very much.
(*enraged, he slams down the receiver*)
I found a place that rents pianos, but they're closing for the day!

PRATT

One thousand two hundred and fifty kiesters, gentlemen, can loll back in that theatre, gentlemen, in comfort and luxury.

TEDDY

How *much*—

MARC

There must be other places . . .

A short silence.

ABE

Come on, Keister, how *much*?

PRATT

(*on his dignity*)

The name is Pratt.

ORSON

(*maniacally cheerful*)

I call him Arnold. He calls me Orson—

HOUSEMAN

You're all getting hysterical—

MARC

Is there a piano?

PRATT

This *is* the Seville Theatre we're talking about?

ORSON

Yes, Arnold.

PRATT

No piano.

PRUETT

A truck.

ORSON

A truck! How right you are, Mr. Pruett. Somebody go find one.

JEANNIE

A truck or a theatre?

ORSON

Darling, we've *got* the theatre—

HOUSEMAN

(*grimly, as he dials*)

Depending on the price—

TEDDY

Let's keep it cool, guys—the truck first, *then* the piano—

ORSON

Jeannie, the first minute you get it—the piano, I mean—phone us here—

JEANNIE

Me—? Just go out and find a truck?

ORSON

She'll need some money, Houseman.

JEANNIE

All I've got is six bucks.

HOUSEMAN

(*much preoccupied with his phone call*)

Good. Whatever you spend we'll reimburse you.

He waves her out with a happy smile. She leaves with great reluctance.

PRATT

A hundred bucks.

Slight pause.

HOUSEMAN

What?

PRATT

Well, Jack, you keep demanding the price—it's a hundred dollars a performance.

HOUSEMAN

We'll take it, of course—

Cheers and congratulations all around.

How much have you got, Orson?

ORSON

I never have more than expense money and Gussie's in charge of it. How much, Gussie?

AUGUSTA

Well, there were all those sandwiches for everybody . . .

HOUSEMAN

We may not be able to get the whole sum together in cash . . . But here—here's my check—

PRATT

Sorry.

HOUSEMAN

No checks?

PRATT

No checks.

CUT TO:

81. EXTERIOR. NEW YORK STREET—TWILIGHT

The tiny figure of JEANNIE can be seen valiantly standing in front of a huge but rickety truck which is ploughing down on her. Luckily the truck squeaks to a stop, and JEANNIE commences negotiations.

TRUCK DRIVER

For me and the truck, lady? Three bucks an hour.

JEANNIE

You gotta deal. Pull up ahead while I phone.

CUT TO:

82. INTERIOR. THE POWDER ROOM

MR. PRUETT

(the phone to his ear, to the others)

It's Jeannie. She's found a truck. But where does it go?

HOUSEMAN

Tell her to keep driving in circles, moving *closer*—

MR. PRUETT

From where?

TEDDY

From wherever she is.

PRATT

(the phone at his ear, turns to the group)

The Mirabelle—a little gem of a theatre—Five hundred seats downstairs, two hundred balcony—and clean, gentlemen—you could eat off the floor—

(interrupts himself, listens to a voice on phone)

Unavailable. The owner's somewhere in Miami Beach . . .

CUT TO:

83. EXTERIOR. THE ROOF OF THE THEATRE—EARLY EVENING

The weather is pleasant. A GROUP OF ACTORS have made their way up by means of the fire escape. The guitar can be heard.

BIG JIM

(a beloved figure in popular Front circles)

That's Will Geer down there, he's going to entertain the public till the doors are unlocked—

MOSES

That figgers to be quite a concert.

VIRGINIA

Let's just hope we finally get something besides those famous fighting songs from the Spanish Civil War.

SHIRLEY

(*a bit sharply*)

Why—?

MAYZIE

Too Left Wing for Ginny.

The others exchange looks.

VIRGINIA

(*very angry and upset*)

Too Left Wing for *now*!

HIRAM

Well . . . who's for martyrdom, and who's for meat and potatoes?

VIRGINIA

I suppose you think I don't know about that.

HIRAM

About what, dear?

VIRGINIA

Well . . . with us it was half a cauliflower. We broke into an empty house, Orson and I—a mansion—an ice box of a mansion. Rolled ourselves up in a rug and that's how we lived. Three days and nights on that lousy, uncooked cauliflower—

MOSES

You were broke, Mamma.

VIRGINIA

You're damned right we were broke.

MOSES

Broke is one thing, down and out is another.

VIRGINIA

Okay, *okay*! I'm the spoiled rich brat who doesn't know the right way to shiver when she's cold. But I know how to worry. And I *do* worry—

MAYZIE

Of course you do, sweetie, nobody can worry better than you.

CUT TO:

84. INTERIOR. MOM AND POP CIGAR STORE—LOWER EAST SIDE—TWILIGHT

JEANNIE on the phone, the head TRUCK DRIVER listening. She hangs up.

TRUCK DRIVER

So what's he say?

JEANNIE

Keep on driving.

TRUCK DRIVER

Look, lady, I got a wife and kids—

CUT TO:

85. INTERIOR. POWDER ROOM

A lot more people have arrived on the scene—all waiting to learn what's going to happen. (HOUSEMAN, a realist, has just about given up.)

PRATT

(to the group)

Victory! The last house on Broadway—That is, for one night at a time—

MR. PRUETT

Sign 'em up.

PRATT

The Dillingham on 49th. They'll take a check—

Enthusiastic applause.

CUT TO:

86. EXTERIOR. STREET—EARLY EVENING

JEANNIE starts out of the truck.

TRUCK DRIVER

You gonna call back again, kiddo, it costs you four more bucks.

JEANNIE

You might even get five.

She says this in attempted lightness, but the TRUCK DRIVER and his COMPANION don't smile.

CUT TO:

87. INTERIOR. THE POWDER ROOM

MR. PRUETT

(picking up the phone)

Yes—?

(to the others)

It's Jeannie. Any news?

TEDDY

We found a place where she can get a piano.

(grabbing the phone)

Jeannie? I'll give you the address—

FRESH ANGLE: ANOTHER GROUP

AUGUSTA

Shouldn't we be checking with the unions?

HOUSEMAN

I'll try Equity one more time—

(he starts to dial)

MARC

And Petrillo—

OLIVE

Who?

HOUSEMAN

(the phone at his ear)

The boss of the Musician's Union. Now I'm calling Equity—

(into phone)

Mr. Gilmore—?

FRESH ANGLE: MARC

MARC

Unions are what "The Cradle's" all about—

HOUSEMAN

(into phone)

When he does come in, please tell him I'll call back.

MARC

(excited)

I should do the talking—I'm the musician.

TEDDY

(into phone)

Okay, Jeannie—? Good . . . Get it loaded on your truck.

CUT TO:

88. INTERIOR. GROCERY STORE—THE TELEPHONE

JEANNIE'S reaction to this last command . . . She has lowered the receiver. Now she raises it to object. But TEDDY has already hung up.

CUT BACK TO:

89. INTERIOR. THE POWDER ROOM

PRATT

I've just checked. I'm afraid the Dillingham is dead.

ABE

(*a great roar*)

Why—?

PRATT

They tore it down.

HOUSEMAN has started dialing.

TEDDY

I'm still worried about Equity—

HOUSEMAN

And I'm still calling them—

OLIVE

Are we allowed to switch managements?

HOUSEMAN

That's the big question.

CUT TO:

90. EXTERIOR. CHEAP LOWER EAST SIDE MUSICAL RENTAL HOUSE—EVENING

JEANNIE'S TRUCK DRIVER and ASSISTANT, aided by two very ancient gentlemen from the rental establishment, carry out an upright piano.

91. INTERIOR. RENTAL HOUSE—EVENING

JEANNIE

(*into phone*)

You still don't have a theatre? So where do we go with the piano? . . .

CUT TO:

92. INTERIOR. POWDER ROOM

Some REPORTERS have joined the scene and are gathered around ORSON.

ORSON

We'll be announcing the name of the new theatre in good time—

The REPORTERS aren't convinced.

As for what we'll use for costumes and sets, or for lighting and musical accompaniment—

MARC

(*cutting in*)

They've closed us down.

CLOSE SHOT: MARC

He hangs up the phone, his face ashen.

ABE

Who says so?

MARC

The Musicians' Union. I couldn't persuade them.

ABE

Screw the Musicians' Union!

(*appealing to the others*)

I've heard it with just Marc at the piano. Even that way it's one helluva show. Can the union stop him from playing his own music?

MARC

They'd throw a picket line around the theatre.

MR. PRUETT

Do they do that with Paderoosky?

MARC

No, but—

(*he breaks off: suddenly struck with an idea*)

A *concert*!

He leaps to his feet. Raising his voice:

There's no thirty-two union men backing up a *concert*— Listen—we're a concert—a *concert*! Do you know what that means? We can use as few musicians as we want to! They can be up on the stage.

HOUSEMAN

But the actors can't.

(having captured general attention with this bombshell)

I've finished talking to Equity. Nobody can appear on any other stage without the permission of the original management.

ORSON

And our "original management" is the United States government.

CUT TO:

93. EXTERIOR. ROOF OF THE THEATRE – EARLY EVENING

SHIRLEY

(a voice of Marxist reason)

Ginny dear – you've just got to learn to think ideologically –

VIRGINIA

(flaring up)

And you've got to learn to call me Virginia –

Another brief pause . . . (from below in the street WILL GEER can be heard still singing.)

BIG JIM

(SHIRLEY'S FRIEND)

Alright, Virginia – what we've got here is a vital issue of censorship: "The Cradle" –

GEATTYS

(breaking in)

Censorship! We could be doing the Life of Jesus, and that same little gang of fascists in Congress would still be putting us out of business.

VIRGINIA

Haven't we been asking for it? Thumbing our noses at them –

BIG JIM

(with his air of intellectual patience)

And what *should* we be doing?

VIRGINIA

We're under fire, aren't we? We should be keeping our heads down –

Groans and moans . . .

The GROUP starts to break up, to move down off the roof by way of the fire escape.

SHIRLEY
(*indignantly*)
So what happened to that beautiful friendship between you and Blitzstein?

VIRGINIA
I love him. And I want his show to open in a proper way, when the Federal Theatre's established as a permanent national institution—

MOSES
(*as he goes*)
Whataya gonna do about Congress? That's where the money comes from.

VIRGINIA
So down will come cradle, baby and all . . . ?

VIRGINIA is almost alone at the top of the fire escape.

Well, Orson is my baby. And this is his theatre . . .

It's the love of his life. And I don't want him to lose it.

CUT TO:

94. INTERIOR. POWDER ROOM

ORSON is on the phone. He's still surrounded by REPORTERS.

FIRST REPORTER
(*shouting*)
It's twenty to seven, Mr. Welles—

ORSON
Yes, and we've got ticket-holders already out there in the street. *They* believe us—
(*into phone*)
Jeannie, darling—you'll just have to work your way closer to us and check in again.

FRESH ANGLE:

TEDDY
Hey! What about the Seville—?

PRATT
Seville?

MARC

Yes, remember? That was the one you said was so perfect—

ABE

Let's get them on the phone—

PRATT picks up the phone and dials.

PRATT

You claimed there was some obstacle.

HOUSEMAN

You did. You said they wouldn't take a check. Suppose we write one for a three-week guarantee? What kind of a gamble will that be tomorrow morning when the banks open?

CUT TO:

95. EXTERIOR. NEW YORK STREET—EVENING

The truck with the piano in it is parked at the curb. JEANNIE, after what she intends as a reassuring word to the two men, goes into a drugstore to phone once again. As soon as her back is turned, the TRUCK DRIVER says something to his ASSISTANT, and they start to move decisively . . .

96. INTERIOR. POWDER ROOM—EVENING

PRATT

(*hanging up*)

They accept.

ORSON

(*raising his voice*)

As you know, we're going to have to get along without an orchestra, stage sets or lighting. And just now an order's come down which seems to say we're going to have to get along without actors—!

Gasps . . . low groans . . . murmur. Reaction.

Don't we have a constitutional right to stand up and sing wherever we'd like to?

The reaction gets hotter.

ORSON (continued)

So it's your decision—you're silent—or you sing.

Big applause.

AUGUSTA

(*turning to HOUSEMAN, her phone at her ear*)

It's Jeannie—

HOUSEMAN

Tell her it's the Seville. Give her the address—

CUT TO:

97. THE THEATRE (891—STAGE DOOR)—EVENING

WILL and HOWARD have broken off entertaining the audience. ORSON and VIRGINIA, followed by LEHMAN, TEDDY, and ABE, come from inside the theatre.

Standing on the raised level which opens on the scene dock (by the stage door entrance) ORSON raises his hands for silence.

ORSON

Thanks for your patience. And now we're going to ask you to participate in something that I don't think has happened in two thousand and more years since people have been going to the theatre.

Low murmur of interest.

What we propose (with your consent) is to move an entire play *with its audience,* on its opening night from *this* theatre to *another* theatre—twenty blocks away.

Surprised and bewildered reaction.

If you're prepared to make that journey—let's call it a pilgrimage—

You're going to the Seville Theatre between 58th and 59th on Seventh Avenue.

But those who think this whole business is as silly as it sounds can have their money cheerfully refunded at the box office. The rest can help to make a little history.

ABE, TEDDY, and LEHMAN are already in the cab. ORSON jumps in. The cab starts away.

97. EXTERIOR. THE THEATRE—EARLY EVENING

The AUDIENCE watches the cab rattle away . . . People exchange looks (this is the moment of decision) . . . A few start in the opposite direction: toward the box office. Then most of them slow up and stop . . .

98. EXTERIOR. NEW YORK STREET—EARLY EVENING

JEANNIE, hurrying out of the drugstore, finds that the truck has vanished. The piano waits forlornly on the street corner.

99. EXTERIOR. NEW YORK STREET—EVENING

The AUDIENCE, marching, four abreast and in high spirits, toward the Seville Theatre.

100. FRESH ANGLE: ORSON'S SPEEDING CAB

ORSON

Hold it!

He has caught sight of JEANNIE'S piano marooned on a side street.

Back up—

They do, and ORSON jumps out calling to JEANNIE as she comes out into the street.

That's beautiful, Jeannie. It's the Seville—just around the corner. Wait, I'll arrange for transportation—

JEANNIE turns to the open archway of the fire department just behind her.

JEANNIE

Don't bother—I've got it under control. Come on, boys—

A number of New York firemen emerge and start grappling cheerfully with the piano.

CUT TO:

101. EXTERIOR. NEW YORK STREET—NIGHT

The marching crowd . . .

102. EXTERIOR. SEVILLE THEATRE—NIGHT

ABE, TEDDY, LEHMAN and ORSON are already at the main doorway which is finally opened by a WATCHMAN in response to their pounding. Too impatient to answer his questions, they force their way past him.

103. INTERIOR. SEVILLE THEATRE

Everything inside the building shows signs of accumulated neglect. ABE and ORSON turn on a couple of lights as they go. ABE makes his way to the stage. MARC comes down the centre aisle joining ORSON.

ORSON
(*quietly*)
I'm sorry, Marc . . . This isn't what I promised you.

MARC
(*looking around, almost in wonderment*)
If it'll work here . . . it'll work anywhere.

ORSON seems to be breathing in the dust of the old playhouse as though it were the bouquet of a vintage wine—profoundly delicious and at the same time exciting, like some celestial drug.

ORSON
You know—just maybe . . .

FRESH ANGLE:

For an instant, ABE FEDER, running through a bank of ancient switches, produces a great flare of light, an intensity matching ORSON'S mood . . .

A blinding burst of flame and the bank of switches blows out.

CUT TO:

104. A FIRE ENGINE SCREECHING PAST THE MARCHING PLAY-GOERS—NIGHT

It pulls up in front of:

105. EXTERIOR. THE SEVILLE THEATRE—NIGHT

A fire engine pulls up . . . JEANNIE, MR. PRUETT and just about everybody else remotely connected with "The Cradle" is riding it with the firemen. Everyone immediately starts trundling out JEANNIE'S piano (which is, of course, the reason for the fire engine) . . .

106. INTERIOR. SEVILLE THEATRE LOBBY

The door of the entrance has glass panes so that some of the light out on the street falls on HOUSEMAN who, with TEDDY at his side, is making his plans—as Homer puts it: "That way and this dividing the swift mind."

HOUSEMAN
That audience was only a few blocks behind us. Somebody should be taking their tickets—

TEDDY

Why bother? The whole place in there is falling to pieces. The switchboard blew out—but Abe's managed to rig up a coupla spots—

CUT TO:

107. INTERIOR. THE SEVILLE THEATRE

ORSON, surrounded by the "Cradle" cast, has just completed some last-minute instructions . . . The actors move to the front of the house. VIRGINIA and HIRAM SHERMAN join ORSON as he moves to the side aisle.

HIRAM

Suppose it *doesn't* work? Suppose it's a mess?

ORSON

The possibility hasn't even occurred to me.

(*turning to AUGUSTA*)

Tell Jack, if it's all right with him, I think we can open the doors now.

(*then, back to HIRAM*)

Do you believe in cycles?

HIRAM

I haven't given it much thought.

ORSON

Seven-year cycles . . .

Seven years ago I stumbled into this profession. The truth is I'm not a fourteen carat theatre professional. I'm an adventurer. So if it's time for me to stumble out, I think I could manage that quite easily.

HIRAM

You know what that is?

ORSON

No?

HIRAM

(*quietly*)

Bullshit.

He leaves the scene.

ORSON

(*to VIRGINIA*)

Well—?

She doesn't speak.

ORSON

Is this the seventh year—or do we wait for the next one around?

VIRGINIA

(*smiling*)

You've still got quite a lot of time.

ORSON

(*a bit sombre*)

It takes a lot of time.

FRESH ANGLE:

MARC

This is a big house, if they're going to hear me in the back we'll have to rip open this piano—

108. EXTERIOR. NEW YORK STREET—NIGHT

The CROWD appears to have increased in size . . . the sound of their feet on the pavement louder than ever . . .

109. INTERIOR. SEVILLE THEATRE

ABE struggling with an ancient spotlight . . . Success! The light goes on.

110. THE STAGE: MARC AND TEDDY

Ripping away the panels from the front of the piano. The house curtain starts to lower . . .

111. EXTERIOR. SEVILLE THEATRE—NIGHT

The front lines of the marching AUDIENCE begin to converge on the theatre . . .

112. INTERIOR. SEVILLE THEATRE (LOOKING TOWARD THE FRONT OF THE HOUSE)

A sudden excited murmur as THE AUDIENCE starts moving through the front doors into the theatre lobby . . . a flicker of flashbulbs . . . The house lights go on . . .

113. SERIES OF SHOTS:

The audience entering, excited . . . Flashbulbs popping.

114. BACK-STAGE:

Peering at the audience through the peephole in the curtain.

115. THE AUDITORIUM:

An impatient, rhythmic clapping starts up . . .

116. CLOSE SHOT: ORSON AND VIRGINIA

MAYZIE enters scene.

MAYZIE
(*into ORSON'S ear*)
Look out—Houseman's going to make a speech.

ORSON
It's quite proper that he should.

MAYZIE
(*after an exchange of looks with VIRGINIA*)
You want people to think he directed this thing?

ORSON
Let's take our seats.

FRESH ANGLE:

On the stage left side three front-row seats have been reserved by means of the ladies' scarves and handbags. Crouching and moving swiftly, ORSON takes the seat on the aisle. VIRGINIA and MAYZIE follow.

117. REVERSE ANGLE: THE STAGE

HOUSEMAN emerges from the proscenium entrance. In the audience the excited chatter falls silent.

118. FRESH ANGLE: BACK-STAGE

Or rather the stage behind the house curtain. MARC sits frozen at his piano. Suddenly he finds ORSON kneeling close to him.

ORSON
Marc—

MARC
Yes?

ORSON
This is where I get off . . . You realize that?

MARC

(*fairly catatonic*)

Just when I need you most.

ORSON

Marc, baby—from here on in you don't need me at all.

MARC says nothing, but it's evident he's unconvinced.

Listen! That thing—

(*indicates the curtain*)

is going up in a few seconds. Right now just tell yourself how much they love you . . .

(*after a beat*)

Jesus! All they're getting is you on this lousy little piano, and more than a thousand of 'em walked twenty blocks for it.

(*another beat*)

Answer this one question honestly, from the bottom of your heart:—Do you really and truly believe that I know more about this . . . stuff . . . than you do?

They hold each other's gaze . . . not an eyelash moves.

MARC

No . . . No I don't.

A CLOSE-UP OF MARC

Transfiguration is too heavy a word, but that's the idea . . . He thinks about it and grows tall . . .

From the other side of the curtain comes a clatter of applause. MARC knows that sort of clapping won't be heard for him.

HOUSEMAN'S VOICE

My name is John Houseman—

CUT TO:

119. THE STAGE:

HOUSEMAN

—the managing director of the Federal Theatre Project 891. "The Cradle Will Rock" by Mr. Blitzstein is an original and distinguished contribution to the American musical theatre. After some two months of preparation, we were abruptly commanded not to open. It was a command we found we could not obey. Mr. Blitzstein's work was ready for an audience tonight. And that is why we are here.

Loud applause . . . Exit HOUSEMAN.

120. BACKSTAGE—THE SEVILLE THEATRE

HOUSEMAN, moving between the proscenium and the house curtian, looks about for TEDDY.

HOUSEMAN
(in a half whisper)
Curtain—! Teddy—bring up the *curtain*—

TEDDY
(coming into scene at HOUSEMAN'S shoulder)
Sorry. Not according to Orson.

121. THE AUDITORIUM—ANGLED TOWARD THE STAGE

ORSON has risen from his front-row seat on the aisle. He stands motionless, leaning against the front of the stage . . . It takes a while for this to register with the excited audience . . . Chatter sinks to a moment's low, busy murmur . . . Then silence . . .

After the silence has focused and belongs firmly to him, ORSON holds it for what almost seems a bit too long. When he does speak it's conversationally—apparently without raising his voice.

ORSON
Marc Blitzstein's opera was written for a large orchestra. The musicians are forbidden to play. Our singers, our actors are forbidden to perform tonight in their own theatre. They are forbidden to stand on any stage, including this one.
(with a faint, slightly conspiratorial smile)
But I understand that most of them came along with you, our audience, on your famous . . . long march.

Laughter.

And if those members of the audience who happen to have rehearsed this show should feel an irresistible urge to stand up where they are, and join in the performance—I don't believe there's any law forbidding that in our free country.
(seriously)
I hope the rest of you appreciate what a risk they will be taking. They earn their living in the Federal Theatre, and they could find themselves tomorrow morning without a job.

Marc's show was meant to have a lot of scenery. But that's all behind us—twenty blocks behind us, and under lock and key. No playwright, no composer since the world began has ever been so lonely.

He's up there, and we're down here—about a thousand of us. But we don't have to just stare at him—

We can keep him company.

He turns, facing the stage . . .

ABE, in the balcony, floods his spotlight so that it fills the house curtain. The bedraggled old thing is suddenly glamorous:—ORSON, still facing the stage, backs up the aisle—Then, when he is out of sight under the balcony, at the back, he calls:

Curtain!

Slowly, a shade jerkily, it rises.

For that time in the theatre what is revealed is the perfect, the Brechtian tableau:

The author-composer (visibly wronged by the establishment) a short, intense, vulnerable figure with short sleeves and suspenders, seated before a small, battered piano on an empty stage.

MARC

The action takes place in Steeltown, U.S.A. on the night of a union organizing drive.

pause.

A street corner, night. Enter Moll.

pause.

Moll sings.

(*after a moment he sings*)

I'm checking home now, call it a night.
Goin' up to my room . . .

Do we hear a second voice?

THE VOICE

. . . Turn on the light.

122. AUDITORIUM

ABE'S spotlight swoops from MARC to the front seats. The dim voice growing stronger now:

OLIVE'S VOICE: Jesus, turn off that light!
I ain't in Steeltown long . . .

CAMERA FOLLOWS the spot as it focuses on OLIVE in the lower left box, pale and frightened-looking.

OLIVE: I work two days a week;
The other five my efforts aren't required.

122. THE AUDITORIUM

The audience is intrigued and delighted with this departure from normal theatrical procedure.

OLIVE (Moll): For two days out of seven,
Two dollar bills I'm given;
So I'm just searchin' along the street.
For on those five days it's nice to eat . . .
Jesus, Jesus, who said let's eat.

A burst of applause.

MARC

Enter Gent.

MARC is ready to speak the lines for this new character, but hesitates while there is even a slight chance that the actor will do it himself . . . He does (rising in the middle of the auditorium).

STANTON (Gent): Hello, Baby.

ABE'S spotlight searches and finds him.

STANTON (Gent): (continued) . . . Busy, baby?

OLIVE (Moll): Not so very.

STANTON (Gent): I'd like to give you a hundred bucks.
But I only got 30 cents . . .

A flare of flashbulbs: newspaper photographers recording a theatrical event.

FRESH ANGLE:

OLIVE (Moll): It was Tuesday last week, yeh, Tuesday.
I had breakfast at Andy's—
Coffee-and; for lunch
I had coffee-and again;
For dinner I could only afford
Coffee. Then I looked on the floor,
And I see a nickel shinin' there. Gee!
(*steps on it*)

Coffee-and, Andy!
Then I looked closer—
That wasn't no nickel.
No coffee-and, Andy, just coffee, Andy—
cute, huh?
Mister, you don't know what it felt like,
Thinkin' that was a nickel under my foot.
(*singing to the melody*
MARC is now playing)
Maybe you wonder what it is,
Makes people good or bad;
Why some guy, an ace without a doubt,
Turns out to be a bastard.
And the other way about.
I'll tell you what I feel:
It's just the nickel under the heel . . .

Oh, you can live like Hearts-and-Flowers,
And every day is a wonderland tour.
Oh, you can dream and scheme
And happily put and take, take and put . . .
But first be sure
The nickel's under your foot.

Big applause.

CUT TO:

123. EXTERIOR. STREET OUTSIDE THE SEVILLE THEATRE—NIGHT

VIRGINIA comes out by one of the fire exits and finds ORSON leaning against a mailbox, smoking a cigar. She moves close to him, and stands there for a while before she speaks.

VIRGINIA

They don't need you in there?

ORSON

Not anymore.

VIRGINIA

But it's a smash.

He doesn't answer. Slight pause.

We'll go back in before it's over? . . . You really ought to.

ORSON looks blank.

You don't want Houseman up there bowing all by himself.

They both laugh.

A stronger volume of sound from inside the theatre catches their attention.

124. INTERIOR. THE SEVILLE THEATRE

(A short part of a scene.)

THEN CUT BACK TO:

125. EXTERIOR. OUTSIDE THE SEVILLE THEATRE

VIRGINIA and ORSON start a short stroll up the street.

VIRGINIA (continued)

First, you know, we *could* try the movies . . . just for a while.

Don't you remember what Sam told us?

ORSON

Sam who?

VIRGINIA

Sam Goldwyn. "For Orson," he said, "I could write a blanket check."

CUT BACK TO:

126. INTERIOR. THE SEVILLE THEATRE

Another part of the play . . .

SERIES OF SCENES:

REACTIONS from our PRINCIPAL CHARACTERS as the performance triumphantly proceeds . . .

All the actors are standing up in their different places in the auditorium . . . A beating of drums seems to be coming from MARC'S magic piano . . . The show is winding up to its finale.

HOWARD: Listen! The boilermakers are with us!
That's the boilermakers' kids—

The Cradle Will Rock is being sung by the chorus—far away at first, then full volume.

HOWARD: The roughers! The rollers! Steel!
Your steel!
They've done it!

MARTY (the cop): They're marchin' down there! They got
no permit to march!

HARRY'S VOICE: Arrest them!

MARTY: Arrest them? There's thousands of 'em!

WILL: My God! What do they want with me?

CUT BACK TO:

127. EXTERIOR. THE STREET OUTSIDE THE SEVILLE THEATRE—NIGHT

VIRGINIA and ORSON, still on their slow stroll, are now on their way back to the fire exit. ("The Cradle" can be heard within)—

VIRGINIA

So how about it? . . .

ORSON

About what?

VIRGINIA

You really think it's time to make your big change in careers? After tonight you've got this town in the palm of your hand.

ORSON

Good time to quit . . .

VIRGINIA

Aren't you just a little tempted by Hollywood?

ORSON

Hollywood is a place where you must never sit down because when you stand up you're sixty-five years old.

(*smiling*)

No, you'll simply have to make up your mind about that divorce.

They stop and turn to each other.

VIRGINIA

That or Washington . . . ? Will I have to kiss a lot of strange babies?

ORSON

That's me. You just have to be gracious.

VIRGINIA

(*after a beat*)

I don't like that joke about divorce.

ORSON

You started it. And it isn't really a joke . . .

(*beat*)

A movie actor—a *divorced* movie actor—as president—? Not a chance.

He opens the fire door—

128. INTERIOR. THE SEVILLE THEATRE

The song starts. The audience has heard it earlier in the show and they join in, singing and clapping in time with the actors and the chorus.

HOWARD (leading it): That's thunder, that's lightning.
And it's going to surround you!
No wonder these stormbirds
Seem to circle around you—
Well, you can climb down,
And you can't sit still!
That's a storm that's going to last until
The final wind blows—
And when the wind blows—
The cradle will rock!

The singing and the music break abruptly and there is silence.

Then (just before there's any chance of applause):

MARC: The cradle will rock!

The packed theatre (with all its standees: the late arrivals from the other Broadway shows who somehow got word of this extraordinary event) have taken MARC'S "opera" to its collective heart. Now, as it comes triumphantly to its conclusion, that huge Niagara roar goes up—that mighty, loving explosion which can be heard but once or twice in a theatre lifetime.

Strangers hug each other, rejoicing in a shared experience which has made them one . . . MRS. CRAM, from the balcony, contributes a joyous blizzard of leaflets: "Peace," "peace," "peace," "peace" . . . Tears stream down happy faces . . .

DISSOLVE:

129. MARC—having just been glimpsed rising delightedly from his little piano in the old Seville Theatre to be dressed in instant glory—is seen now from on high, and from some distance, bent over much the same sort of piano . . . For the great artist there may be roses and applause, but mostly there's the steady, ceaseless labor of the honest workman . . .

END TITLE

"The Cradle Will Rock" has played many hundreds of times in much the same manner as its opening night.

Leonard Bernstein was the first, among others, to take the composer's place at the small upright piano.

Marc Blitzstein is sorely missed.

This film is dedicated to him with much affection.

AFTERWORD

by Jonathan Rosenbaum

It somehow seems fitting that in order to piece together Orson Welles's autobiography, we have to turn to his creative work. The unceasing desire and energy to produce that coursed through the seventy years of his life, and literally kept him occupied until his final moments, crowded out the opportunity to recount his life in tranquility, at least in any complete form, yielding only a series of tantalizing fragments. There's a moving account in *F for Fake* (1973) of how, in Dublin at the age of sixteen, he launched his professional career as an actor, and *Filming* Othello (1979) describes how, in Morocco in his mid-thirties, he launched his career as an independent—as opposed to studio—film-maker. A series of extended interviews with Peter Bogdanovich in the late 60s and early 70s—*This is Orson Welles: Conversations* (Harper Collins, 1992)—fill in some other parts of his life story, and a film project he worked on intermittently over the last decade in his life, *Orson Welles Solo*—a sort of scrapbook self-portrait for which he filmed conversations with his old friends Roger and Hortense Hill in 1978, and wrote two brief autobiographical fragments about his parents, "My Father Wore Black Spats" and "A Brief Career as a Musical Prodigy" (both published in the Christmas 1982 issue of the French *Vogue*)—fill in a few more. Very shortly before his death, he began writing an autobiography in earnest, but never got beyond a few pages.

Perhaps the most extended and complete of his autobiographical ventures was written in 1984, the year before his death, and it came about quite by chance. If, as Welles often pointed out, a film director is someone who "presides over accidents," the "accident" that brought about this protracted exercise in self-scrutiny—an original screenplay called *The Cradle Will Rock*—is no less striking than the series of chance occurrences charted in the script itself.

Producer Michael Fitzgerald, whose features at this point included two John Huston pictures, *Wise Blood* and *Under the Volcano*, had commissioned a first-draft screenplay from Ring Lardner, Jr., *Rocking the Cradle*, which dealt with the events surrounding Welles's 1937 stage production of Marc Blitzstein's "play with music," *The Cradle Will Rock*.

Fitzgerald then showed this script to Welles in June 1984 for his approval, and over the course of their ensuing discussions, invited Welles to direct the film himself. After showing some initial reluctance about the project (see Barbara Leaming's *Orson Welles* for details), Welles wound up not only agreeing, but completely discarding Lardner's script and writing a new one himself—turning the film in the process into an autobiographical account of his life during the first half of 1937, just before and after he turned twenty-two. (In Lardner's script, Welles was a less central figure—certainly a less developed one—and the emphasis was placed more squarely and exclusively on the production of the Blitzstein play.)

Insofar as this period constituted the time just before Welles achieved his biggest fame—he appeared on the cover of *Time* Magazine on May 6, 1938, less than a year after *The Cradle Will Rock* opened—the script can be said to describe an existential point in his career that may have been even more decisive than any of his subsequent adventures in Hollywood, Latin America, or Europe. Indeed, precisely because this pivotal moment is virtually lost today to those who assume that Welles's career "began" with *Caesar* on the stage (November 11, 1937), *The War of the Worlds* on radio (October 30, 1938), and/or *Citizen Kane* in film (May 1, 1941), Welles's focusing on it here carries the force of a resurrection—the summoning up of a forgotten past that implicitly affects our sense of everything that came afterward. Following on the heels of another original screenplay by Welles, *The Big Brass Ring*—written in 1981-82, and published posthumously by Santa Teresa Press in 1987—*The Cradle Will Rock* might be said to bear some of the same relationship to its predecessor as *The Magnificent Ambersons* has to *Citizen Kane*: after a flamboyant and fearless speculation about corruption, a modest and highly self-critical reflection on the brashness of innocence, tinged with sweetness and nostalgia.

Significantly, *The Cradle Will Rock* was by far the most "directorless" of Welles's stage productions, and in order to ferret out the overall meaning it had in a career that is known mainly for its individuality, it becomes necessary to arrive at an understanding of the overall political and social context in which Welles flourished during the late Depression. As Michael Denning has argued in an essay that has direct bearing on this issue,* "If the Mercury project is representative of the popular front, their productions may be read as allegories of their contradictory populism, a populism worth reexamining in the midst of our own debates over the politics of that contemporary embrace of the popular which has been called postmodernism."

* "Towards a People's Theater: The Cultural Politics of the Mercury Theatre," *Persistence of Vision* no. 7, 1989.

For Denning, the premiere of *The Cradle Will Rock* constituted the first of two events "that prevented the Mercury from becoming merely an avant-garde theater group, from being a radicalism of special effects" — the other event being "the panic caused by the radio broadcast of *The War of the Worlds*" the following year. "The evening [of the *Cradle* premiere] marked the end of Welles's and Houseman's connection to the Federal Theatre; and its notoriety launched the Mercury Theatre that fall. And it served as an emblem of what Houseman and Welles meant as a people's theater, which was less an ideological theater — though despite Houseman's latter-day disclaimers, they shared what Gramsci would call the 'common sense' of the popular front — than a theater marked by a new and wider audience." As Blitzstein himself noted at the time, in a piece written for the *Daily Worker*, "*The Cradle Will Rock* is about unions, but only incidentally about unions. What I really wanted to talk about was the middle class." For all its trappings as a proletarian labor opera, *The Cradle*, which Blitzstein dedicated to Bertolt Brecht, was specifically conceived as a Marxist work that addressed itself to the bourgeoisie.

Furthermore, if we agree with Denning that ultimately, the "Mercury went from an experiment in people's theater to a trademark for a star," the brief period covered in the *Cradle* screenplay might be said to be the period when the ambiguities of that contradictory evolution were most apparent — ambiguities that, judging from the screenplay, weren't entirely lost of Welles himself. One thing, for example, that clearly distinguished the Welles-Houseman projects for the Federal Theater — and which serves to account for the fact that they succeeded in forging more productions through the WPA bureaucracy than all the other theater groups — was the fact that they illegally drew funds from Welles's lucrative career during this period as an anonymous radio actor. (It could be argued, indeed, that part of the scandal of Welles's iconoclasm throughout much of his career — encompassing not only the period covered in *Cradle*, but such later maverick film productions as *Othello*, *Don Quixote*, and *The Deep* — was his willingness to subsidize substantial portions of his own work.) Such details as the political ambivalences of Orson and Virginia about their upper-class habits and attitudes, Orson's reference to his uncollected WPA salary (which was actually $23.86), and his changing an effect in *Dr. Faustus* with the use of a mirror in order to make room for Blitzstein's rehearsal piano, should all be seen in light of the particular conflicts and negotiations provoked by *The Cradle* between Welles's political and entrepreneurial drives.

For conceptual insights into what sort of film Welles wanted to make from his script, Welles's young friend Jim Steinmeyer—a magician he met in the early 80s, saw on the average of once a week, and discussed *The Cradle Will Rock* with at length—has been especially helpful. About a year and a half prior to the *Cradle* script, Welles had already discussed with Steinmeyer a possible film project about magic shows at the turn of the century, and their common interest in magic proved to have more relevance to certain aspects of *Cradle* than might first seem apparent. As Steinmeyer put it to me, Welles wanted to present himself in the film as a magician on Broadway.

Take, for instances, the backstage and behind-the-scenes basement glimpses of Christopher Marlowe's *The Tragical History of Dr. Faustus* that are witnessed by Marc Blitzstein towards the beginning. Welles recalled *Dr. Faustus* to Steinmeyer as an "all black-art show," a production whose magical effects were centered on lights and curtains. Discussing with Steinmeyer the relationship between events on the stage and events under the stage, Welles wanted to convey the *impression* that the under-the-stage operations "explained" the onstage magic without its actually doing so. He didn't feel, moreover, that he had to represent the original *Faustus* production faithfully. In the original, there was a scene featuring "The Seven Deadly Sins" that consisted of Bil Baird's puppets and floating objects, including a pig, that were moved around invisibly by stagehands dressed in black. Although a pig played a minor role in this scene, it wasn't a pig that was big enough for an actor to ride. For the very elaborate, "borderline-impossible" floating pig trick in the movie—which Welles wanted to shoot in Rome for economic reasons, and which was designed and built by John Gaughan—a number of shifting principles were involved. Steinmeyer declined to go into further details about this (too many of the principles are currently in use by other magicians), but stressed that "black art" wasn't involved: the trick would have been performed in bright light.

Steinmeyer recalls Welles saying that the script remained the most important aspect of the film to him; theoretically it could have been directed by someone else. The most important thing about the casting for him was getting actors who looked like the original people. (Some of the actors he contemplated using at various points were David Steinberg as Marc Blitzstein, Amy Irving as Virginia, Jackie Mason as Moishe the cab driver, and David Ogden Stiers as John Houseman; Stiers having studied with Houseman and observed him firsthand was a particular incentive.)

Entertaining some doubts about how Blitzstein's *Cradle* might play for a contemporary audience, Welles lent an audiocassette of the opera to Steinmeyer; when his friend reported back that he didn't like it much, Welles sadly agreed that the play was dated and said that he would endeavor (in Steinmeyer's words) "to write circles around it."

In the August 30 issue of *Variety*, Todd McCarthy reported that production manager Tom Shaw was "lining up locations and crew for [a] moderately budgeted production" that would require ten weeks of shooting, with nine weeks in Los Angeles for interiors and another week of second-unit work in New York. John Landis and George Folsey, Jr. were slated as executive producers and Michael and Kathy Fitzgerald, assisted by Prince Alessandro Tasca di Cuto, were announced as "line" producers. Ted Pedas's Circle Theaters—an 8-screen movie theater chain in the Washington, D.C, area—were cited as the source of financing, and McCarthy added that English actor Rupert Everett was cast in the part of the young Welles.

According to Tasca, the initial budget was $6 million, and the shooting locations and facilities that had been pre-figured by the fall—while Welles worked on revising his script in October and November—included a still wider range of possibilities: one theater south of Long Beach and two theater interiors in Rome, Italy (one of them a cinema called the Olympico); exterior locations in Staten Island and Hoboken as well as downtown Los Angeles; possible studio work in Los Angeles (without union crews) and/or Utah; and studio work for the film's country house interiors in Rome. The film would be shot on color negative (as a commercial safeguard) but processed in black and white.

But by the end of the year, the expected financing failed to materialize; and what began as a hopeful postponement eventually became a regretful cancellation a few months before Welles's death on October 10, 1985—even after the budget had been reduced to $3 million and various European investors had been sought. (Another story in *Variety*—dated May 31, 1985 and filed from Munich—reported that the film, now allegedly called *Let the Cradle Rock*, "may begin within a year's time," with Hans Brockmann of Anthea Films co-producing with Michael Fitzgerald, and shooting to take place entirely in Europe.)

When Welles, in one of his last-ditch efforts to save the project, invited Steven Spielberg and his then-wife Amy Irving (tentatively cast as Virginia Nicholson Welles) to lunch at Ma Maison, there might have still been some cause for hope. Spielberg, after all, had recently spent $55,000 at an auction for the Rosebud sled in *Citizen Kane*, and according to Welles biographer Frank Brady, Spielberg's *Indiana Jones and the Temple of Doom* had even more recently grossed nearly $10 million in a single day.

Perhaps Welles assumed that even if Spielberg didn't want to invest in *The Cradle Will Rock* himself, he could lend a helping hand in other ways simply by picking up a phone; surely he had the clout to get *someone* to invest $5 or $6 million in what would have been the first Hollywood studio film by Welles in a quarter of a century, ever since *Touch of Evil.* But as Welles discovered to his regret, Spielberg didn't even offer to pay for the lunch. (This story, incidentally, has been confirmed by Welles's daughter Beatrice, to whom Welles recounted it later the same evening, in Las Vegas.)

Other friends or acquaintances in the industry were scarcely any more helpful. When Warren Beatty invited Welles to lunch at the same restaurant, asking him to bring the *Cradle* script with him, he insisted on reading the script straight through at the table while Welles sat waiting for him, then offered the suggestion that Welles shoot present-day interviews with surviving real-life participants in the original events—in short, imitate Beatty's own procedure in *Reds*. . . . A couple of studio reports that I've read on the *Cradle* script seem characteristic: both readers complain that the script assumes an interest in Welles's early life that they didn't happen to share.

Far from anything like a settling of old accounts—a frequent motivation for show-biz autobiographies—Welles's look back at his own youth is full of generosity towards others and more than a few skeptical notions about his earlier self, including his marital infidelities and his sexual double standard. Significantly, Virginia Nicholson both read and approved the screenplay during the preproduction, and even Welles's old enemy John Houseman—who read it after Welles's death and not long before his own—commented favorably on its overall fairness and accuracy.

It should be stressed, however, that Welles felt free to adopt a certain poetic license when it came to handling a few specific historical events, as well as some personal ones. A more precise chronology reveals some of the alterations:

Spring 1936:	Blitzstein writes *The Cradle Will Rock.*
Fall 1936:	Blitzstein meets Welles backstage during the run of the latter's production of *Horse Eats Hat* to discuss Welles directing *The Cradle* for the Actor's Repertory Company. (Soon afterwards, the project is put aside due to lack of funds.)

January 8, 1937:	*Dr. Faustus* opens.
March 1937:	Houseman and Welles decide to produce *The Cradle* at the Maxine Elliott Theater for Project #891 and rehearsals begin.
May 9, 1937:	*Dr. Faustus* closes.
May 23, 1937:	John D. Rockefeller dies.
May 30, 1937:	Ten Republic Steel strikers are killed by the Chicago police.
June 1937:	Technical rehearsals on *The Cradle* begin, despite massive budget cuts in the New York Theatre Project.
June 12, 1937:	The production of *The Cradle* is prohibited by government order.
June 14, 1937:	Final dress rehearsal for hundreds of invited guests.
June 15, 1937:	A dozen uniformed guards take over the Maxine Elliott Theatre.
June 16, 1937:	The play is performed at the Venice Theatre.
December 1938:	Texas Representative Martin Dies asks Hallie Flanagan, head of the Federal Theatre, if "this Marlowe" is "a Communist."

Not all of Welles's characters in the script can be verified by other accounts of the period, so it seems possible that a few of them — including Solly Pruett, Moishe the cab driver and Mayzie Katz, among others — are either fictionalized composites or pure inventions. (We have it on good authority, however, that Mrs. J. Sargeant Cram "really existed," as Welles's narration insists.) There's also a likely telescoping of some of Welles's future interests in Hollywood and presidential politics in the final dialogue with Virginia.

Perhaps the most telling calculated departure from history in the script is the name of the theater where the *Cradle* premiered, which was actually called the Venice rather than the Seville. (Subsequently, the same theater was renamed the New Century, then the 57th Street.) In fact, Welles gravitated between calling the theater the Venice and the Seville in separate drafts of the script; Tasca has a script dated November 1984 which calls the theater the Venice, but his call-sheet for the production lists it as the Seville. Like the question of whether Blake Pellerin or Kim Meneker murdered the blind beggar at the end of *The Big Brass Ring*, Welles's uncertainty about this matter, probably based on his autobiographical associations with both cities, evidently carried some potency for him; as his companion and collaborator Oja Kodar pointed out to me when I brought this matter up, "Orson sometimes liked to invent his own superstitions." (A line from movie director Jake Hanneford in the script of Welles's still-unreleased *The Other Side of the Wind*: "Seville. That's one of the great places. Venice, Ankorvat, the God-damned Pyramids – they're all so many used-up movie sets.")

Negotiating the complex truces between fiction and nonfiction is a daunting task throughout Welles's work, largely because the *Cradle* screenplay is far from being the first time that he works with a fictional or nonfictional character named Orson Welles. Throughout his radio career, for instance, one finds him sharing the same narrative space as his fictional characters. In his radio version of *Huckleberry Finn* (broadcast on March 17, 1940), there are extended dialogues between "Huck Finn" (Jackie Cooper) and "Mr. Welles"; in his own controversial radio play *His Honor the Mayor* (broadcast on April 6, 1941), where he functions as narrator, he remarks at one point of his hero Bill Knaggs (Ray Collins), the mayor of a town near the Mexican border, "Believe me, I'm not campaigning for Knaggs's re-election. He's a friend of mine, but I don't want to get mixed up in municipal politics, particularly in a town that's almost 2,000 miles away from my own." In 1944, on the variety show *Orson Welles Almanac*, there are even many times when he converses at length with the Disney character Jiminy Cricket.

After the triumphant premiere of Blitzenstein's *Cradle*, the show reopened at the Venice in the same impromptu form two days later, where it played through July 1st. During the same period, it was given an extra Sunday performance at an amusement park in Bethlehem, Pennsylvania and a performance in Uncasville, New York before touring the steel districts of Pennsylvania and Ohio. On June 27, New York radio station WEVD – named after the socialist hero Eugene V. Debs – broadcast it. On December 5, the show was revived in a new "oratorio version" at the Mercury Theatre (formerly the Comedy Theatre, on 110 West 41st Street) on Sunday nights, utilizing the *Caesar* set, two rows of chairs, a reduced chorus of twelve, and Blitzstein himself resuming his original role at the piano. When Random House published the text of the play the following year, Welles began his Preface by saying, "I started producing Marc Blitzstein's music drama the minute it was written almost two years ago, and I have been producing it almost incessantly ever since."

Welles and Blitzstein collaborated on many subsequent occasions over the next two decades, especially during the late 30s. Five months after the *Cradle* opened, Welles's next stage production, *Caesar*, featured music by Blitzstein; the composer performed the same role on Welles's production of *Danton's Death* a year later, and also did the music for the Mercury Text Records of *Julius Caesar* and *Twelfth Night* released in 1939. On February 8, 1938, Welles hosted a benefit concert for *New Masses*, during which Blitzstein's half-hour "song play" *I've Got the Tune*, dedicated to Welles, received its stage premiere (with Count Basie performing in one section), and Welles arranged for the piece to be performed at the Mercury on two Sundays later the same month. In mid-July, Blitzstein played the part of a French barber in the film shot by Welles for his production of the stage farce *Too Much Johnson*. Eight years later, when Blitzstein's *Airborne Symphony*, a cantata for male voices, premiered at the New York City Center, Welles served as the narrator. And ten years after that, in 1956, again at the New York City Center, Blitzstein was in charge of the music for Welles's last American stage production, *King Lear*, and played the harpsichord during its run.*

Indeed, considering the symbiotic and reciprocal nature of this friendship over the years, it might not be too fanciful to consider Blitzstein's character as a sort of alter-ego of Welles in the script. (In this respect, Welles as scriptwriter may have been only returning the compliment. Welles was originally cast by Blitzstein as the composer, Mr. Musiker, in the autobiographical *I've Got the Tune* for its CBS radio premiere in October 1937, and Blitzstein wound up taking over the part himself only after Welles proved to be too busy rehearsing *Caesar*.) For all the political differences between these characters, one could argue that Blitzstein not only influenced Welles, but eventually, in certain respects, came to stand for a significant part of his artistic persona—his political conscience and consciousness—over the remainder of his career.

In "The Director as Actor," a paper delivered by James Naremore at a Welles conference in Venice, Italy in October 1991, there is a passage that pinpoints precisely the dual artistic persona that I have in mind: ". . . I would argue that Welles's major accomplishment as both an actor and director was his ability to synthesize two apparently contradictory forms of theatricality: On the one hand, he was a brilliant practitioner of what John Houseman called 'magical effect,' and he was clearly indebted to a romantic or gothic tradition of Shakespearian drama, grand opera, and stage illusionism; on the other hand, he was also a didactic, somewhat Brechtian storyteller whose cultural politics were shaped during the period of the Popular Front, and whose technique was visibly rhetorical,

---

* See Eric A. Gordon's biography *Mark the Music: The Life and Work of Marc Blitzstein* (New York: St. Martin's Press, 1989) for a comprehensive account of Blitzstein's career.

strongly dependent on direct address. The tension between these extremes—in other words, the tension between Welles as conjurer and Welles as narrator—accounts for many of the special qualities of his films in general."

Naremore goes on to cite *F for Fake*—where Welles "appears as a narrator-magician, and where he behaves like a cross between a pedagogue and a con man"—as a prime example of this duality. Very much the same duality is present at the first meeting between Blitzstein and Welles—a Brechtian pedagogue and a magician on Broadway—in *The Cradle Will Rock*, defining a kind of friendly ideological tension that continues throughout the script. A similar friendship of symbiotic opposites is defined between Welles and Jack Carter, and it's worth adding that Welles actually *did* replace Carter in black face in the voodoo *Macbeth* during at least part of its run in Indianapolis in 1936. But if Carter literally played Mephistophilis to Welles's Faust, and if, according to Houseman, Welles himself was also Mephistophilis to his own Faust, it's less certain in the friendship between Welles and Blitzstein precisely who was Faust and who was Mephistophilis. Each clearly inspired the other to do things he never would have undertaken otherwise, and this screenplay shines with the fond memory of what happened when their mutual inspiration took the world by storm.

ORSON WELLES, a master of theater, radio and film, is perhaps best remembered for his groundbreaking work in all three media: *Julius Caesar* (1937), *The War of the Worlds* (1938) and *Citizen Kane* (1941), respectively. His other films include *The Magnificent Ambersons, The Lady from Shanghai, Macbeth, Othello, Mr. Arkadin, Touch of Evil, The Trial, Chimes at Midnight, F for Fake* and the still unreleased *The Other Side of the Wind.*

JAMES PEPPER is the editor of such film books as *"Chinatown" A Screenplay* by Robert Towne, *Raymond Chandler's Unknown Thriller: The Screenplay of Playback,* Philip Dunne's screenplay book of *How Green Was My Valley,* and Harry Carey, Jr.'s *Company of Heroes: My Life as an Actor in the John Ford Stock Company.*

JONATHAN ROSENBAUM is film critic for the *Chicago Reader,* translator of the book *Orson Welles; A Critical View* by Andre Bazin, and editor of *This Is Orson Welles* by Orson Welles and Peter Bogdanovich; he also contributed an Afterword to Welles's original screenplay *The Big Brass Ring.* His own books include *Moving Places: A Life at the Movies, Midnight Movies* (with J. Hoberman), *Greed,* and *Placing Movies: The Practice of Film Criticism* (forthcoming).